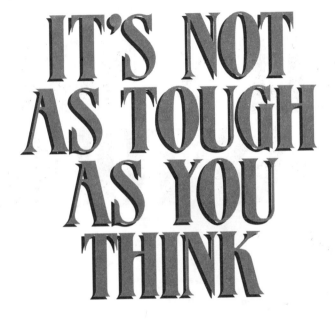

IT'S NOT AS TOUGH AS YOU THINK

IT'S NOT AS TOUGH

A
SHAAR
PRESS
PUBLICATION

AS YOU THINK

How to Smooth Out Life's Bumps

RABBI ABRAHAM J. TWERSKI, M.D.

CONTENTS

INTRODUCTION

Life has always been full of challenges. In earlier days man had to escape from wild animals. Today he has to escape from oncoming traffic. Prior to the amazing scientific and technologic advances of recent times, there were many hardships in life. In the modern world, many of these have been eliminated. Instead, we have air and water pollution that threaten the very existence of life.

Human beings have great adaptability. We can confront and overcome many challenges. Our coping skills are diminished, however, if we are in a negative state of mind.

Very often things are nowhere near as bad as they may seem. At other times things may indeed be bad, but we can lift ourselves above them and go on with what we must do in life. Either way, our mood is a determining factor in our capacity to function optimally.

Some things in the world are changeable, others are not. Our mood is always changeable. The more positive our attitude, the

13

more effective is our ability to modify some things, and the greater is our ability to accept other things.

I hope that the pages ahead will foster a more positive attitude. We can then be both happier and more productive.

~

I gratefully acknowledge the valuable contribution of my daughter, Sarah Twerski, R.N., in the editing of the manuscript. Her comments have enhanced the messages I have tried to convey.

1.

MAY YOU HAVE MANY WORRIES

Life is full of annoyances. You open your washing machine and discover that all your whites have a blue hue, because somehow a dark-blue sock was mixed in with the load. Or you rush downtown to take advantage of a spectacular sale, only to find that there are enormous bargains to be had — in every size but yours. Or you turn the key in the lock and it breaks off, and your husband, who has the other key, is away on a business trip. There are minor annoyances or major annoyances. Obviously you become irritated, but how much irritation is justifiable?

On one of my trips to Israel I visited a friend, and asked him to pray at the Western Wall for my brother, who was ill with cancer. As I was leaving, he said, "May you have many worries."

I was taken aback by this remark. "What kind of blessing is that?" I asked.

My friend explained, "You see, it is impossible for there not to be *any* annoyances and irritations in life. Nothing ever goes completely smoothly . But if there is no single problem that is overwhelming, then we are bothered by a number of things that upset us. If there is one problem that is extremely grave, it obscures every other annoyance, and we are focused totally on that one major problem.

"Right now," my friend continued, "you are so concerned about your brother's illness, that nothing else bothers you. That is why having only one problem or one worry is not good, because it means that this one problem is terribly serious. If you have many worries, that means that nothing is so bad that it drives away all the rest, and that is about as good as life can be."

So next time you are irritated — as, for example, it is late at night, say, 1 A.M., and your automobile alarm goes off, and you are simply beside yourself — just think. Aren't there other things on your mind? Perhaps you just got the bill from the dentist for your son's braces, or there was water in the basement from the heavy rains this week. If you have any kind of normal life, you should be able to find a few other irritations. Then give thanks to God that you have many worries. God forbid you should have only one worry! The car alarm going off is not the end of the world by any means. It will shut off and resolve itself, just as the other worries — if there are many — will be resolved in one way or another.

Some psychologists may teach you how to relax by expelling an irritating thought from your mind. My friend suggests another method, one which is much easier to accomplish and at far lesser cost: Bring in a few more worries, and then feel relaxed precisely because you have so many.

BEHIND AT HALF TIME

I once attended a meeting of recovering addicts at which a young woman described her downhill course from adolescence through early adult life. Fortunately, she eventually came to her senses and joined a recovery group, which enabled her to emerge from the torment of her addiction.

After she gave a brief resume of her life history, she stated, "There is one more thing I would like to tell you."

"I am a rabid football fan, and my team is the New York Jets. I will never skip watching a game. One time I had to leave town for the weekend, and I asked a friend of mine to record the football game on her video.

"When I returned, my friend gave me the video cassette, and said, 'Oh, by the way, the Jets won.'"

"I began watching the game, and the Jets were falling far behind. By half time, they were trailing by 20 points. At other times, I would have been pacing the floor, wringing my hands, and possibly raiding the refrigerator. However, I was perfectly calm, because I knew that my team was going to win, hence there was no need for me to worry.

"Ever since I turned my life over to God, I know that it is going to turn out good. There may be some hitches on the way, but I know that God will not fail me.

"Sometimes I feel like I am trailing by 20 points at half time, but since I know that the end will be good and that I will overcome and succeed, nothing ever upsets me as it did before."

If our faith is strong enough, we can be winners, and even if we might be trailing at some point, we should approach the future with confidence.

WHO WANTS TO BE MARRIED TO A LOSER?

It may seem inevitable that two people living in close contact will have some disagreements. Sometimes these disagreements lead to arguments. While some quarreling between husband and wife may not be serious, at other times some unkind words are said in the heat of the dispute, and these may inflict emotional pain. It is not always easy to maintain full control of one's words, and either intentionally or unintentionally one may say something that is derogatory or that strikes a raw nerve. It would be best if reasonable disagreements could be discussed without their degenerating into arguments.

This is easier said than done. Marriage counselors are kept busy trying to restore communication between spouses. I was fortunate to hear some words of wisdom, which, if given due consideration, may avert some of the more common problems in marriage.

"My wife and I used to argue," this man said, "and I would be defensive and do anything necessary to make my point. My ego could not tolerate losing an argument to my wife.

"Then one day it occurred to me that if I won the argument, she lost it, and then I would be married to a loser. Well, I didn't want to be married to a loser, so we stopped arguing."

We usually think of ego as indicating self-centeredness. Perhaps self-centeredness is not always bad. In this case, this man's ego could not tolerate either winning or losing an argument, and the only choice was to quit arguing.

Give this some thought. It may save your marriage.

4.

IT ALL DEPENDS ON HOW YOU SEE IT

In the villages of the old country, many people were illiterate, and if they needed to write a letter they would go to the town scribe. One woman, whose son had immigrated to the United States, had not heard from him in several months, and asked the scribe to write a letter for her. She dictated as follows:

Dear Son,

I'm sorry that I have not heard from you for several months. Please write me and let me know how things are going for you.

With me, things are quite well. We have had a difficult winter, and the cold wind would come through the crevices in the walls, but thank God, I was able to seal the crevices with some old garments. The price of food has gone up very high, but thank God, day-old bread is much cheaper, and I can afford this. I still have my house-cleaning job, and thank God that at my age I am still able to do this kind of work.

I am anxiously waiting to hear from you.

Love, Mother

The woman then asked the scribe to read what he had written. The scribe, who was outraged at the son's neglect of his mother, wrote as follows:

Dear Son,

What in the world is wrong with you that you have not written to me? Conditions here are intolerable. The icy wind blows through the crevices of the walls and I have to try and stuff them with rags. I can't afford proper food, and I have to eat day-old bread. At my old age I still have to get on my hands and knees to scrub floors in order to survive. This is the kind of life I am leading here while you seem to be enjoying yourself in America.

When the scribe finished reading the letter, the woman grabbed hold of her head with her hands and said, "*Oy vay!* I never knew how bad off I was until now."

It is not always necessary to change conditions. Sometimes all that is needed is a change in perspective.

5.

WHERE DO THE CHECK MARKS GO?

Few parents have a completely smooth course in raising their children. There are several excellent texts that can serve as guides on child rearing. We would be wise to give serious consideration to how we relate to our children, rather than responding reflexly. We are not born as scholars, lawyers, or computer programmers. These require intense training. Why, then, do we assume that we are all born competent parents? Parenting is the single greatest and most far-reaching responsibility we have. Would it not be wise to prepare ourselves adequately for this challenge rather than rely on intuition and knee-jerk reactions?

One simple suggestion can bring rich rewards. We often catch our children doing something wrong and we chastise them, whereas we tend to take for granted everything that they do right, and we do not acknowledge this. If Michael leaves his jacket on the floor, he is likely to hear, "Pick that jacket up off the floor and hang it up where it belongs!" On the other hand, when he does hang up his jacket, he may not hear, "Thank you for hanging up your jacket. That was thoughtful of you." Similarly, when Sarah puts the dishes into the sink, she may not be told, "Thank you for helping clean the table," but if she walks away without doing so, she is likely to hear, "What do you think this is? A restaurant?"

Someone has remarked that there is an unspoken attitude conveyed to children, beginning in grade school. Their test papers are generally returned with check marks that indicate which answers are *wrong* rather than marking those that are *right*.

There are many things our children do every day that are right. It would enhance our relationship with our children as well as elevate their self-esteem if we validated these behaviors. Our attitudes should not be one-sided. Let us remember to try and "catch" our children doing something good *three times a day* and acknowledge it.

False compliments and flattery are of no value, but acknowledging something done properly reinforces positive behavior. Both parents and children stand to profit from this.

6.

IF ONLY YOU KNEW MORE, YOU MIGHT NOT BE SO FRUSTRATED

You know what it feels like when you are late for your appointment with the dentist, especially since he commented on it when you were late last time. Well, this time I was going to give myself plenty of time, just in case the road was blocked by a jack-knifed tractor-trailer. But don't you know, that's when the air-conditioner repair service came, for whom I had been waiting in the sweltering heat. Thank God it was just a minor thing, and if there was no tractor-trailer blocking the road, I could still make it in time.

A long funeral procession is not as bad as a tractor-trailer, but I sat in the car fuming. I was going to be late. Why do people have to die at an inconvenient time? When the two hundredth car finally passed, I drove in a frenzy — as if that would make any difference. O.K., five minutes late is no calamity (I hope the dentist agrees).

I drove into the parking garage, knowing that at this time of the day I would be lucky to find a space on the eleventh floor.

Ahead of me were two cars, crawling at a snail's pace. My goodness! What's wrong with that first car? What does he think this is? Relaxing after a hearty meal? The car in front of me was tooting his horn. I was going to do likewise, to urge that slowpoke in front to move on. But what good would two horns do? Just make more noise. So I did nothing.

Eventually the lead car pulled into a space, and it was then that I noticed the handicap symbol on the license plate. That's why he was going so slow! Thank God I did not toot my horn. I would have been consumed with guilt.

Sure, I felt frustrated and furious as I crept along behind those cars, but if I had only known that the lead car was driven by a handicapped person looking for a suitable place to park, I would not have been tormented by anger and frustration.

Now, when I feel I am getting frustrated, I think , "Maybe there is something I don't know, and if I only knew more I would not be so upset." I find that I can unwind much more easily. Try it.

7.

YOU WANT TO BE HEARD, DON'T YOU?

Sometimes we are provoked. No, that's not quite right. We are provoked *frequently*. Sometimes the provocations are minor, sometimes major, and sometimes they are really minor but appear to be major. But it makes no difference. Minor or major, we generally get angry when provoked, and we may act out our anger in shouting or gesturing.

Many times our anger is completely justified, and we have every reason to express our displeasure or reprimand someone for his dereliction. I assume that what we wish to do is to get our message across that we are displeased with what was done, and especially that such mistakes should not be repeated. It is therefore important to know that when we scream or gesticulate, the message often does *not* get across. When you begin to shout, people may tune you out. Sure, they will be impressed and remember that you were angry, but the content of the message may have been lost. Sometimes people become defensive when you start screaming, and instead of realizing that they were wrong, may insist that they were right.

The Talmud states it simply and beautifully: "An angry person accomplishes nothing other than being angry" (*Kiddushin* 41a). Solomon says, "The gentle words of the wise are heard" (*Ecclesiasties* 9:17). Absolutely true. When you speak softly, people will listen. When you are in a rage, you accomplish nothing.

So you come home after an exhausting day at work, and the kids have left their jackets strewn all over the place, they are fighting with each other, and when you walk into the kitchen you realize that there had been a tornado that apparently went unreported. "These kids don't know how to listen. Unless I scream my heart and lungs out at them they totally ignore me." That's what you may think, but let me assure you, if they don't listen when you talk calmly, they will be even less attentive when you scream.

It is not easy to restrain yourself when you have been disobeyed for the umpteenth time. Nor is it easy to remain calm when you lost a lucrative contract because someone failed to do what he was supposed to. The point is conceded. But what is your wish? To discharge anger (which, by the way, doesn't work) or to get things done right? If you really want the latter, then count to ten, or take a mouthful of water and hold it for a while before you react.

I once had as a patient an executive whom I had to teach how to relax because he was experiencing chest pains from tension.

One time I called to change an appointment, and his secretary said, "Doctor, whatever you are doing with him, do more of it. It is a pleasure to work for him." He was accomplishing much more with a pleasant tone than when he tyrannized the office.

Try it. Watch what happens when your demeanor changes. You'll be surprised that even the kids will listen.

8.

AVOID THE NEED FOR REGRETS

I know it is not pleasant to think about it, but the fact is that no one lives forever. Hopefully, we will be mentally alert at a ripe old age, and it is very likely that we will review the period of time we spent on this planet.

What are the chances you will say, "My only regret is that I did not spend more time at the office?" If you do, you will enter the Guinness book of records as the first person in the history of mankind to say that. Everyone else says, "I wish I had spent more time with my family." Some people say, "I wish I had spent more time learning Torah." Well, why not think ahead and lead your life in a way that you won't have these regrets?

Yes, the office is important. That is where you earn your livelihood, and that is where you try to earn enough so that you can give the kids the things they need. But wait a minute! Have you ever thought that one of the things the kids need most is *you*? If you are not spending enough time with the children because you are busy trying to earn more in order to buy them *things,* you are making a loud statement that "things are more important, more worthy, more valuable to you than I am." If that is the way you feel about yourself, that appraisal may be communicated to the children. I would not be surprised if the kids pick up your attitude and begin to think that things are indeed more important than you.

Thank God for the Sabbath day. Without it the kids might not even know who we are!

I am not so foolish as to underestimate the things that are the necessities and even some of the niceties of life. But that still does not justify spending a lopsided amount of time at work relative to how much time we spend with the family. So do readjust your priorities, and spend more time with the family and with studying Scripture. You will develop a feeling of emotional well-being that will be beneficial to everyone. And you won't have anything to regret.

9.

FUTILE ACTIONS ARE FUTILE

It's not easy to keep your wits about you when you're under stress. Unfortunately, when a fire breaks out in a theater or other gathering, more people are injured by the trampling as people try to run out in panic than by the fire. If people were only able to avoid going out of their minds with fear and file out in an orderly fashion, many lives otherwise lost would be saved. But when we smell smoke or someone yells "Fire!" all logic is lost, and people rush for the door.

This can happen to an individual as well as to a group. However, an individual has a better chance of acting rationally, because his anxiety is not aggravated by the group reaction.

The shortest way from my home to my office involved going down a steep hill. In winter, if the hill was icy, the police would set up barricades to block access. I would drive by, and if the barricades were up, I would take an alternate route.

One time I drove by and there were no barricades in place. Assuming that the hill was safe, I drove down it. The police must have overlooked it that day, because the hill was treacherously slippery. My car began to slide out of control. I pumped the brakes, to no avail. I tried to steer the car into the curb, but the wheels would just not respond. At the bottom of the hill there was a busy thoroughfare, and I knew I was going to be killed when my car would come to the intersection at the bottom of the hill. I furiously kept pumping the ineffective brakes and turning the non-functioning steering wheel. It was only because God wanted me to live that my car slipped through the thoroughfare without being demolished by traffic from both sides. But I had no knowledge that I would be saved by a miracle, and it was obvious that my life was about to come to a violent end.

In retrospect, the logical thing for me to have done was to open the door and jump out. The car would have proceeded downhill empty and been destroyed, and I would probably have suffered one or more broken bones, but at least I would be alive. But instead of doing what was logical to save my life, I kept on frantically pumping the brakes and turning the steering wheel, both of which were very obviously not working.

Unfortunately, stress may sometimes be so severe that we cannot avoid panicking. However, if a stress is not imminently life-threatening, we should be able to retain our logic so that we may do something that can help rather than engage in futile behavior. It might help if we would periodically say to ourselves, "I must remember to avoid knee-jerk reactions." By keeping ourselves aware of this, we may be able postpone a reflex reaction to a provocation or other stressful situation, until we have enough time to think it over and act according to reason rather than to blind emotion.

10.

IT MAY BE VERY BIG

There is a wonderful little book, *Don't Sweat the Small Stuff,* which provides some excellent advice on how to deal with many of the stressful or frustrating situations that we encounter in daily life. However, its subtitle, *and it's all small stuff,* is not always applicable. There are some things in life that are not at all small, and may be very big indeed.

If someone loses a loved one, that is a very, very major stress. If someone loses everything they own in a fire or flood, that is very big. If someone learns that his child has a serious illness, that is indeed huge. These can in no way be considered "small stuff."

Yet, we must also learn to cope with these major happenings, because there are only two ways to deal with a stressful occurrence: 1) Cope with it, or 2) escape from it. Escape is sometimes the proper choice, as when the building is on fire. But there are times when escape is inappropriate. Escape from the loss of a loved one? Whereto? Into alcohol? The relief of alcohol lasts only as long as the oblivion lasts, but then the stress returns in full force, unless, of course, one chooses to stay drunk and oblivious for the rest of one's life.

Escape into suicide? Do we really own our lives that we are free to dispense with them? Furthermore, shall we inflict terrible pain on others because we are in distress? Is that not cruel? Is it fair to compound one mistake by making an even greater one?

No, there is no escape from many major stresses, and the only other option is to cope with them. But how?

First we must accept the reality of the situation. If we deny it and make believe it did not occur, we get absolutely nowhere. We may be angry, and legitimately so. We may be angry at our employer, at the reckless driver, or even at God. The Talmud states that a person is not held accountable for his anger at God when he is in agony (*Bava Basra* 16b). But what good will anger do? It will not change things in the least.

Since we are not going to kill ourselves, we have no option other than to adjust to the world, unfair as it may be. At this time, the support of friends is crucial. No, they cannot change reality, but it has been correctly stated that "a sorrow shared is a sorrow halved." It is particularly helpful to share with people who have had a similar experience, and who can share their strength, hope, and courage. There are a number of "self-help" groups that attend to specific stresses, and their help is invaluable. A sensitive clergyperson can also be of assistance. And even people who were intensely angry at God nevertheless found strength and solace in prayer.

These are things we must sweat, because we have no other choice.

36

11.

TAKE THINGS IN PERSPECTIVE

There is just no way to get through life without many irritating things happening. You may recognize some of these as rather trivial and have little trouble getting over them, but there are some annoyances that are more substantial and can really get you upset. Having a proper perspective can help.

Let's suppose you have been buying lottery tickets, and one day, voilà! The numbers picked today were yours! Can this be true? You pinch yourself. No, you're not dreaming. It has really happened! Still in disbelief, you call up to verify the numbers, and you check the numbers and date on your ticket, and there they are! You are now a millionaire, and with 3 million dollars you will be able to do so many things you had only dreamt of; that you can't even begin to count them. A dream come true.

You're on the telephone telling your wife the great news, and in your haste you knock over the lamp, which shatters into smithereens. Unfortunately, it was a Tiffany lamp, quite expensive, and you had a great liking for it. But what of it? What is the loss of a few hundred dollars to a millionaire? You don't even give it a second thought.

Of course, if this lamp had been broken at any other time, it would have really grieved you. A beautiful and expensive lamp, which you could not afford to replace. You really would have felt bad, and probably brooded over it for who knows how long. But now, the loss of the lamp pales into insignificance compared to your windfall winnings.

Each morning I recite a series of blessings, thanking God for my eyesight, for being able to get out of bed, for having clothes, for being able to walk, and for His giving me energy. I recite a blessing for the coffee I drink, the bread I eat, and I thank Him for the food He provided, and my ability to eat it.

We really should be grateful for every breath we take, and for being able to think. There are countless things which should elicit profound gratitude.

We should not take all of these things for granted. They are gifts, and we are so fortunate to have them. There are some people who do not have the things that we take for granted. All those things are far more precious than even winning the lottery, and it is a mistake not to recognize this.

All right, so something has gone wrong. You sustained a loss or suffered some discomfort. How much would you brood over this if you have won the lottery the very same day? Well, you have won even more than the lottery. You can breathe, see, hear, eat, walk, talk, and get dressed. You are a winner! So of what significance is the disappointment you have experienced?

Certainly no one wishes to be an ingrate. Brooding too much over an unpleasant incident may indicate that we are unappreciative of the gifts we have received.

12.

JUDGE FAVORABLY AND ACT ACCORDINGLY

W hen my son was Bar Mitzvah, I met a friend from whom I had not received an RSVP (I must confess that I myself am guilty of not responding speedily to invitations). "I haven't received your reply yet," I said. My friend retorted, "If I would have received an invitation, you would have received my answer," and I detected a note of resentment in his voice.

I was stunned. I distinctly remembered having addressed an invitation to him, and I was certain that he would attend. Later the same day I discovered that the psychiatrist who was my supervisor during my residency had likewise not received an invitation. Since my friend's last name began with "P" and my supervisor's with "R," I suspected that somehow the "P's" and "R's" had been mislaid or lost in the mail. I checked with others in these categories, and discovered that, indeed, they too had not received invitations. I called all the "P's" and "R's" and apologized, and asked them to please attend the Bar Mitzvah.

Ever since, if I do not receive an invitation to a friend's affair,

I do not feel slighted. I assume that what happened to my "P's" and "R's" may have happened to my invitation. I therefore go to the reception uninvited. Inasmuch as I realize that my friends have not made arrangements for me to attend, I do not stay for the meal, but I am there for the Bar Mitzvah or wedding ceremony. I extend my congratulations and best wishes to the family, and in every case, the hosts have expressed their gratitude for my attendance.

If you know you belong at someone's festivities but have not received an invitation, go anyway. Don't stay for the meal, since they have not counted on this, but convey your congratulations and best wishes to the host and other family members. You and they will both be glad you did so.

13.

STAY WITHIN REALITY

It is true that there is nothing beyond God's capability, and indeed, many extraordinary miracles have occurred. This notwithstanding, the Talmud tells us not to rely on miracles. While we should always pray for Divine help, we should stay within the confines of reality. Thus, if one's wife is expecting, the husband should not pray that his wife have a boy/girl, because since the child's gender is already determined, such a prayer is futile.

Two youngsters were conversing and one said, "If you could have anything you wanted, what would you wish for?"

"I'd wish for a sandwich," the second boy said. "I'm hungry."

"That's foolish," the first boy said. "Why, I'd wish for a million, gazillion dollars and my own space shuttle, my private continent, three horses, and a fancy sports car."

A bit later the friends met again, and the second boy was eating a sandwich. "I got *my* wish," he said.

Yes, we must pray, and we should even dream, but both

prayer and dreams should be within the confines of reality. Our aspirations should be for things we can realistically achieve by our own efforts, blessed with Divine assistance. However, dreams and prayers for the absurd are futile.

The Talmud states, "If you reach for things within reason, you may get them. If you seek things that are clearly beyond your abilities to achieve, you will end up with nothing (*Rosh Hashanah* 4b). So, do pray and dream, but stay within reality.

14.

AGED WINE IS SUPERIOR

Getting along in years has its problems. As you grow old, people begin to mumble in an undertone which is barely audible, the telephone directories use smaller print, you can tell when the weather is going to change without listening to the radio, and your memory becomes moth eaten. As they say, the only redeeming feature about growing old is that *not* to grow old is a worse option.

But as with wine which improves with time, aging does have its advantages.

I remember when the baseball player, Andy Pafko, was in his last year in the game. At age 45 one is considered a senior citizen in sports. Andy was playing right field for the Braves, when the batter hit a ball that was certainly destined to be a homerun. With his back against the wall, Andy jumped and caught the ball, saving the game for his team.

The sports announcer went bananas with this fabulous catch, and in his ecstasy he said, "Just imagine! At age 45 he could still make a jump which we could expect only of much younger athletes."

His fellow announcer commented, "No, you're wrong. Perhaps a younger man has quicker reflexes and stronger muscles, but only someone with many years of experience would know just when and exactly how to jump to catch that ball. A youthful and much more agile player might be able to jump higher and faster, but only someone like Andy could know exactly how to place himself and jump to make a catch like that."

He was right. Youth certainly has nimble skills, but these may not be enough to do the job. The wisdom of years of experience may more than compensate for the youthful strength, spirit and speed.

This may only be the defensive thinking of someone pushing 70, but somehow I don't think so.

15.

RUN FOR YOUR LIFE

The salutary effects to the heart and circulation which result from jogging are well known. It is logical that teaching the heart to pump efficiently can strengthen it. But why would jogging have a good effect on emotions? Listen to this.

Some psychiatric researchers encouraged a group of depressed patients to jog every day. There was another group of patients with similar symptoms who were treated with antidepressant medication. Both groups had relief of their depressive symptoms to the same degree!

Why is this? Probably because the adrenalin hormone or other substances released during jogging accomplish the same restoration of the altered body chemistry as the antidepressant medication. I have not seen a similar report on swimming, but I have anecdotal reports from people who said that their depression improved with swimming.

Why then is it necessary to use antidepressant medication? Because many people with depression cannot be motivated to jog or swim, certainly not to the degree of vigorous exercise necessary for the relief of symptoms.

However, most often we are not severely depressed. Rather, we may be "out of sorts," perhaps mildly depressed for known or unknown reasons. If one could push himself to jogging or swimming, there is a great likelihood that his mood will improve significantly. As a bonus, he will be improving his circulation, and strengthening his heart and muscles. That, too, should make a person feel better.

So, in more ways than one, Run for Your Life!

16.

LIFE EMULATES PRAYER

There are three recurring themes in prayer: (1) We thank God; (2) we express our love for God; and (3) we express our regret for the wrongs we may have done, and ask for forgiveness.

Someone once asked a wise rabbi, "Are my prayers really heard?" The rabbi replied, "Do you listen?"

There are several areas of communication in which we often find some resistance. Some people find it difficult to express their gratitude, and in fact they may have some difficulty even in acknowledging gratitude. This can be seen even with young children, when the mother's plea, "Say 'thank you' to the nice man for the candy," is met with a grunt. There may be even greater resistance to admit one's wrong action, apologize, and ask to be forgiven. This too seems to be an inborn trait, in that children will adamantly refuse to say, "I'm sorry," and apologize. Finally, whereas young men and women during courtship repeatedly acknowledge their deep feelings for one another, this often comes to an abrupt halt with the marriage ceremony, and the verbal expression of affection may be rarely heard throughout their married life.

How wonderful it would be if we overcame our resistance, and more frequently expressed our gratitude, affection and regret for having done wrong!

One of the advantages we should derive from prayer is that these ideas should become more familiar to us, and as we verbalize to God, it should then become easier for us to say them to people. We must listen intently to our own prayers. Indeed, the Talmud says that "A person who is pleasing to other people is also pleasing to God." Refining our behavior refines our relationship to God.

How many marriages might have been preserved if only the spouses had more often said these three simple phrases to each other: "I thank you," "I love you," and "I'm sorry, but I was wrong."

17.

LOSING CAN BE WINNING

An associate tells of the following experience:

This was a very important occasion for me. I was to deliver the keynote address at a National Women's Convention in Chicago. The opening session was in the evening, and I had an important meeting in New York which I had to attend. But there was ample time for me to catch a plane that would get me to Chicago early enough to freshen up and get to the convention.

Inasmuch as this occurred in June, I had no reason to suspect any weather delays, but just in case there might be a mechanical problem that might cause a delay, I checked with another airline. In the event there was any trouble with my flight, I had a back-up flight. I had covered all bases, or at least I thought I had.

My flight took off on time and arrived in time, but then the unforeseen happened. My suitcase did not arrive, and my dress and shoes were in that bag! I panicked, and had the airline baggage service trace it. It was indeed safe and sound in New York, and it would get to Chicago on the next flight. They promised to deliver it to the hotel.

The next flight! By the time it arrived and was delivered it would be way too late! I was beside myself! I was not going to get up on the stage in the dress I was wearing. No way! There was no purpose in my hanging around the airport any longer, so I took a taxi to the hotel, berating myself all the way for being so stupid to check in the baggage that held the dress. I should have taken it in a garment bag as a carry-on.

At the hotel, I ran into some of my friends and told them of my terrible plight. One of them suggested, "There is a department store just two blocks away. Why don't you see if you can get a dress there?" I had no better idea, and so we rushed over to the store.

Would you believe it? I tried on a very elegant dress that looked as if it was made to fit me, and it was on sale! I also found shoes to match. Best of all, the airline was responsible for this, and would pay 50 percent of the cost.

I delivered my speech in a dress which earned me some flattering comments. I bought it at a bargain price, and 50 percent of that was covered by the airline!

What a blessing! And to think that I had panicked and brooded over what I had felt was a tragedy.

I am fortunate in that every time I wear that dress, I am reminded of how short sighted we may sometimes be, and not recognize a blessing when it occurs.

18.

THERE MAY BE SALVATION IN A CRISIS

Like a bolt of lightening, a crisis can be illuminating.

A young man consulted me. His wife had divorced him after the first year of marriage. They had run into trouble early in the marriage because of his inability to govern his anger, and he had been very domineering and controlling. "I couldn't see that there was anything wrong in what I was doing. I loved and respected my father, and I followed his pattern. He was the boss in the house, and my mother accepted and loved him, anger and all. When we went for marriage counseling and my wife complained about my behavior, I could not understand why she was not accommodating like my mother was. I was not cooperating in the marriage counseling, and when she served me with divorce papers, my attitude was, 'Good. I don't need a wife who is so obstinate.' There were no children, and I did not contest the divorce, which became final a few weeks ago. I went back to live with my parents, but this time I can see how wrong and destructive my father's behavior is. I know I am much like him, and unless I change, I will wreck the next marriage as well. I know I need help in changing myself."

It is not uncommon for us to emulate our parents and to think that the way they act is normal and correct. If this young man's wife had been like his mother and had tolerated his abusive behavior, he might never have discovered that it was dysfunctional. The divorce actually brought him to his senses.

When I was in medical school, we were taught that it may often be necessary to dilate a patient's pupils in order to see the eyegrounds. We were instructed to always have a syringe of morphine available, because if the patient had undetected glaucoma, dilating the pupils could precipitate an attack of acute glaucoma, which is extremely painful. Our instructor said, "But do not hesitate to dilate because of fear of precipitating an acute attack of glaucoma. You will actually be doing the patient a great favor by revealing that he has glaucoma, because this can be treated. If it is not discovered and goes untreated, it could result in a loss of vision."

There is no question that an attack of acute glaucoma is terrible, yet it may save the patient's vision. This is equally true of many other crises. In the case of the young man, the crisis of the divorce "saved his vision." He had not been able to *see* that his father's behavior, although tolerated by his mother, was very wrong. He could now *see* that he had copied his father's behavior, and that he must make changes in himself if he wished to have a healthy relationship.

If we learn from a crisis, we maximize an opportunity for growth.

19.

THE SAGA OF THE SALMON

It is not always easy to follow the proper course in life. Sometimes our environment is not conducive and may even be frankly antagonistic to Torah principles. It is not unusual to find that we must overcome major obstacles to remain faithful to Torah. Today, it is not too difficult to be a Sabbath observer, but I remember the days when it was difficult to find a job that would allow a person to be off on Saturday, and many people had the fortitude to overcome this challenge to their faith in order to observe the Sabbath. This was equally true of many other aspects of religious life, which often posed major challenges.

I visited a salmon fishery on the west coast, and it is nothing less than awesome to watch how the salmon battle the current and swim upstream to get to their spawning place. When they encounter a cascade, they jump high to get to the next level. If they fail to negotiate the leap, they swim around a bit to renew their energy and then try again, doing so repeatedly until they succeed.

The salmon's behavior is dictated by instinct. They "know" where they must go and they make certain that they get there, even though they have to swim against a strong current and leap over numerous cascades. There is no stopping them, and they do not surrender in the face of the obstacles in their way.

Humans do not operate primarily by instinct, but rather by intellect. We are instructed by the Torah as to what we must do, and we must carry out our assignment regardless of how difficult it may be. Yes, our environment may exert a strong pull, but we may have to resist this pull and make our way "against the current." There may be formidable obstacles along the way, and not infrequently our attempt to overcome them results in failure. However, we are not to become frustrated and surrender. Rather, like the salmon, we must revitalize our energy and try again and again until we succeed.

God gave the salmon the strength to carry out its instinctive drive toward its goal. He has also given us the strength to achieve our goal and to overcome any and all of the challenges that may stand in our way.

20.

NOWADAYS IT'S TOUGHER

Although the theme of this book is to realize that we have the capacity to cope with all of life's challenges, and that with the proper perspective things may not be as difficult as they seem, we should also be aware that sometimes things are tougher than they seem. This is especially true of raising children.

Parenting has gone on since creation, and if we think back to our own formative years, we may see that although our parents may not have had the easiest chore in raising us, it was nevertheless not a formidable task. We may therefore think that we, too, can raise our children without too much exertion. This is not true.

The world has undergone some radical changes in the past few decades. In the '60s, the startling achievements of science led man to think that he was infinitely wise and in total control of his own destiny. The worship of the genius of man led to the concept that "God is dead," and religion suffered a setback. Along with this came a defiance of all authority and a rejection of hallowed principles. "Do your own thing" became the common byword. The unbridled pursuit of pleasure resulted in a devastating epidemic of drug use. Violence spread like wildfire, and previously unheard-of senseless aggression, far worse than that of brute beasts, has been exhibited by young people and even children. The culture has surrendered to some of man's basest drives by legalizing them.

This is not the world in which our parents and grandparents were raised, and not even that in which we were brought up. But it is the world into which we bring our children, and it is nothing less than a formidable task to teach children the principles of decency and morality.

While this is not an impossible task, neither is it one which we can achieve by coasting along. In previous times, children who received their cues from the street were not in great danger, because the street was quite decent. Today the street is toxic, and we must help our children resist its impact.

Unless we realize the full scope of today's challenges to our children, we may fail to exert the requisite effort to help them grow up as decent and truly dignified human beings. We may need to study techniques of successful parenting and consult with those who are competent to provide us with the skills that will enable us to raise our children properly. We must have a greater understanding of the ethics of living as set forth in Torah writings.

For our parents and grandparents, raising children may not have been all that tough, and we may have a false sense of security that things are still the same. This is one time when we must realize that *this* task is tougher than we may think.

21.

WE ARE NEVER ALONE

Small children are often afraid of being left alone, and may howl and put up a fuss when the parent leaves the room. This may occur even if the child has never experienced a traumatic incident that might justify this fear. It seems that the fear of being alone may be a basic, inborn feeling, and this fear may persist into adulthood and even throughout one's life.

There are, of course, circumstances when a person is alone. In the past, the stability of the community and the family militated against isolation, but in today's mobile society, aloneness is much more common. A widow or widower who has three children and lives in Chicago may not live near any of them, because one lives in Seattle, the other in New Orleans, and the third in Boston. The neighbors with whom one was friendly for many years may have moved to Florida. These circumstances may result in a person being deprived of close relationships. For the elderly, the problem may be accentuated by their inability to get around, because they may no longer be able to drive, and the wear-and-tear diseases of aging may even make it difficult for them to walk, resulting in their becoming "shut-ins" in their apartments.

As unpleasant as such solitude may be, it is surpassed by the aloneness that one feels when depressed. In this case, one tends to feel not only alone, but what is much worse, abandoned. People who may have experienced some type of abandonment in their childhood are particularly vulnerable to such feelings if they become depressed, even many decades later.

Rabbi Nachman of Breslov writes extensively about his depression, and states that there were times when he felt he was in the deepest recesses of hell. Yet, he never felt abandoned, because he recalled the verse (*Psalms* 139:8), "If I ascend to the heavens, You are there, and if I descend into hell, You are there too." Since there is no place bereft of God, He is everywhere, and His presence accompanies even those who are in the depths of hell. The knowledge that God was always with him banished the frightening feeling of aloneness and abandonment and gave him a modicum of comfort in his anguish.

Of course, when one feels alone, having someone nearby whom one can see and touch and who can respond is highly desirable, but this is where our faith is indispensable. We must know that God is always with us.

22.

THERE'S MAGIC IN A SMILE

I was at a medical conference, and sitting across from me was a doctor who had his thumb and forefinger at the corners of his mouth, and every few moments moved the corners of his mouth upward as if smiling. He noticed that I was looking at him and said, "This is not a neurotic tic. I came across an article which said that not only does the emotion of a smile lift your spirits, but even the muscular action involved in forming a smile can make you feel better. I tried it, and it works. Today is the kind of day that I don't have anything to smile about, so I fabricate a smile by pushing up the corners of my mouth."

At first I thought this guy was way out, but afterward I decided, "What do I stand to lose?" So on days when I am not particularly cheerful, I smile as though I was cheerful. It may not make me feel elated, but it does make me feel better.

While life is a serious business, a cheerful attitude can enable us to cope much more effectively. Rabbi Aaron of Karlin said, "The Torah does not say that feeling dejected is sinful. However, feeling dejected can lead a person to the most severe sinfulness."

The renowned sage Rabbah would introduce his lectures with something that would make his students cheerful, following which he began expounding on Torah with the utmost reverence. Rabbah knew that an upbeat attitude is conducive to better learning.

Our great Torah personalities were able to maintain an attitude of joy even under the most trying conditions. They were fully capable of wit and good humor, which they felt was essential to avoid the pitfall of dejection.

Hopefully, you will have much to smile about. On days when you do not feel like smiling, smile anyway. A smile can alleviate sadness without any side effects.

23.

A MOVE IN THE RIGHT DIRECTION

A young woman consulted me, very upset because she had repeatedly tried to lose weight, and finally had adhered to a weight control program for a full year, and then relapsed. She felt she was a total failure and was back to square one, having accomplished nothing.

I told the young woman that one day during a winter frigid spell I had to send a registered letter. However, my car would not start and I knew it would be hours before I would get service. Since the post office was only six blocks away I decided to walk there. I watched my steps on the icy sidewalk, but after three blocks I slipped, getting bruised but fortunately not breaking any bones. I arose and walked the rest of the way, this time being much more on the alert for slippery spots.

If anyone had said that because I slipped and fell I was back at my home, they would clearly be wrong. The fall did not erase the three blocks progress I had made, and I was halfway to my destination. As a result of the fall I became much more cautious to prevent it from happening again.

I told the young woman that her relapse did not erase the progress she had made by disciplining herself for a whole year. She was not at all back to square one. She had learned much about controlling her eating habits, and although she had slipped, the progress she had made was important. She could now try to identify why the slip had occurred and avoid a similar slip in the future. Like my fall on the ice, the slip was a learning experience.

Whether the problem is smoking, drinking, compulsive eating, or any other behavior which had gone out of control, any period of success is a gain. Setbacks are unpleasant, but we can survive them and learn from them. If you suffer a setback, remember two things: (1) It should alert you to do whatever is necessary to avoid falling again, and (2) the progress you had made cannot be taken from you. It is dangerous to take a defeatist attitude, because then one may resign oneself to failure. The fact that one had maintained discipline for an extended period of time is incontrovertible evidence that one can do so. If one can do it for a year, one can do it for fifty years.

24

DON'T GET PARANOID

I was quite young when I took my first position as a rabbi. I had become quite adept at public speaking, and before too long the word got out that my sermons were something special.

There were several rabbis in the city who had held their positions for many years. On one occasion I was on a panel together with an older rabbi. He spoke in a monotone, and although the content of what he said was good, his delivery left much to be desired. When my turn came, I included a few stories and some one-liners. The response of the audience to me was clearly more enthusiastic than their response to the other rabbi, and it seemed to me that he felt slighted because this young kid had upstaged him. I promised myself I would not do that again.

One day I was called to co-officiate at a funeral. The man who died had attended our synagogue on occasion, but was also a member of the other rabbi's synagogue. He had been very active in many community projects and had many friends; hence it was expected that there would be a huge attendance at his funeral. Because the other synagogue's social hall was much larger, the family decided to have the funeral service there.

The host rabbi began his eulogy, and after a few minutes the public address system failed, and no one beyond the first few rows could hear anything. Someone went out to get the maintenance man, but by the time the problem was corrected, the eulogy was almost over, and it was my turn to speak. My eulogy was heard by all.

But what if it had been the other way around? What if the public address system had failed in the middle of *my* sermon? Who would have been able to convince me that this was not a deliberate act because the host rabbi was annoyed with me and did not want me to upstage him again? I would have been absolutely certain of this, and would never have believed it was an accident. I would have been very angry, and I would have borne a grudge against the other rabbi.

Well, it did *not* happen in the middle of *my* sermon, but in the middle of *his*, so it was clearly an accident. Since that time I have avoided jumping to conclusions when something happens that I could interpret as being directed against me. The Talmud says "Always judge a person favorably" (*Ethics of the Fathers* 1:6), and this incident has helped me to do so.

You may think that something that is annoying to you may have been done deliberately. Take it easy, and don't get paranoid. It may well have been purely accidental.

25.

TRUTH IS STRANGER THAN FICTION

The Talmud says that a person's actions are rewarded in kind, measure for measure. The following true story is an example of this.

In 1952, two young boys, David and Jacob, found a bankbook with $150 in cash, a very significant sum in those days. They took it to the bank, which contacted the owner. The man was overjoyed and he gave the boys $20 as a reward. Knowing that their school was in dire straits, the boys donated the money to their school. The bank president thought this was newsworthy, and reported it to the newspaper which published it as a human interest story.

The two boys, who were close friends, eventually parted ways and lost contact with each other. Forty years later, David was going through some old mementos, and came across the newspaper article. "What ever happened to Jacob?" he wondered. He looked in the local telephone directory, and called several people who had the same last name, but no one knew of Jacob.

He searched the Internet and wrote letters to people all over the country who had the same last name, but to no avail.

After a good deal of searching, he found that Jacob had a distant relative, and after a long and arduous course, Jacob was located in a distant city. David called him, and the long-interrupted friendship was renewed. They arranged to meet, and they spent many hours reminiscing about events of their youth, including the episode of finding the bankbook. They parted with a promise to stay in contact and not let the friendship of their youth wither away.

One week later, Jacob called David, all excited. "You won't believe this," he said. "I went into a store to buy something, and when I reached for my wallet, it was gone. I had a large sum of money in it, and it was a major loss for me. When I came home, the light on my answering machine was blinking. The message was from someone who had found the wallet and wished to return it to me."

David responded, "You remember what we learned in school, that God acts towards us as we act towards others? Sometimes it may take 45 years for this to come about, but God always keeps his promise."

Sometimes we may think that our good deeds are not necessarily rewarded. We may just need a bit more patience.

26.

FIRST THINGS (BIG THINGS) FIRST

In daily living we must distinguish between what is major and what is relatively minor, because otherwise we may spend our time on trivia and neglect major items. Neither our time nor our energy is infinite, and we must prioritize.

An instructor once demonstrated this to his class. He took a wide-mouth jar and filled it with rocks. "Is this jar full?" he asked. "Of course," the students responded. He then took fistfuls of gravel and put it in the jar, pointing out that the jar had not been full, and that there was room for the gravel. Then he put some sand in, which found its way to the spaces between the gravel, and finally he added water, which filled all the spaces in the jar. "You see," he said, "by putting the rocks in first, there was room for everything. Had I put the smaller objects in first, I could never have gotten the rocks in."

If at the end of the day or the end of the week you find that you have been left with much work undone, it is a good idea to review how you prioritized your time. If the big things are taken care of first, you may well be able to get everything done.

27.

TOLERATING SUSPENSE

As we have seen, not everything is "small stuff," and we need all the help we can get in coping with the "big stuff."

One woman was told that the sonogram indicated a defect in her fetus: One arm ended at the elbow. Since terminating the pregnancy was out of the question, she resigned herself to this, and upon researching found that many things can be done to augment the limb to approach normal function.

However, the woman also realized that if there is one defect in the fetal development, there may be others that are not detectable by the sonogram, such as heart malformation. The presence or absence of other defects would not be known until the child was born. What if there were defects that required open heart surgery, or perhaps deafness or blindness? How would she adjust to such a challenge? The possibility of what awaited her began to torment her, and she would have to live in this suspense for four more months.

Inasmuch as there was nothing she could do now, she reasoned, "I am obligated to do whatever is in my power. When something is beyond my ability, I must turn it over to God. I will gain nothing by fruitless worry, and whatever challenge I will have to face, I will do it then, not now." She prayed every day, not for God to make her baby whole, but that He give her the strength to cope with whatever eventuates.

The baby was born with the limb defect as seen in the sonogram, but otherwise completely normal. The woman was overjoyed, and proceeded to raise the child to maximize his potential. Had she submitted to the anxiety of the suspense, she would have dissipated her energies and would have compromised her ability to care properly for the child.

We may not know why things like birth defects happen, nor why other adversities occur. Futile worry is self-defeating. We must pray for the strength to cope adequately with whatever we encounter in life, and be secure in the knowledge that God will give us that strength.

28.

THE NARROW BRIDGE

In my home we often sing the melody set to the words of Rabbi Nachman of Breslov, "The whole world is but a narrow bridge, but the important thing is not to panic."

This is easier said than done. I once walked over a rope bridge that spanned a gap which was hundreds of feet deep, and when I looked down, I could not overcome the feeling of intense fear. I had only one solution, to hold on to the railing and look up at the sky rather than down at the deep gorge. Intellectually, I knew that the bridge was safe. Thousands of people had crossed it, and some actually enjoyed the experience. But my intellect could not control my emotions. If I looked down, my feet froze and my heart beat rapidly, and the laughter of those brave souls in front of and behind me did not quash my anxiety.

This may be the way to implement Rabbi Nachman's teaching. The world may sometime be frightening. Things may happen that cause us great anxiety, and if we continue to look at the particular stressful happening, our anxiety may only increase. Even if people around us seem to be navigating the rough waters of life, that may not be of much comfort to us. The solution: Lift your eyes to heaven. Look up to God for support and salvation. Look away from the ordeal, and reinforce your faith and trust in God.

Yes, you may take a pill to reduce your anxiety, but taking a pill has the risk of your developing a false sense of reality, and not heeding your steps. You would be much wiser to "hold on to the railing," to the many kinds of support available, and look up to heaven. You will cross the bridge safely.

Even though we may be able to avoid "sweating the small stuff," we may not be able to control our sweating when "big stuff" occurs. I can testify that I did break out in a sweat when I looked down at the deep gorge beneath the rope bridge. But when I looked up toward the heaven, my anxiety considerably lessened.

29.

A SOBER PERSPECTIVE

A recovering alcoholic said, "I naively expected that when I stopped drinking, everything would go smoothly. This was not the case, and I had many setbacks. But eventually I recognized a pattern: Every setback was a prelude, and sooner or later was followed by something good. Now, when something bad happens, I get excited about the good that is going to come about, and I can't wait to see what it is." This is a sound philosophy, but sometimes we can see this only in retrospect.

We spent one Sabbath with our children, returning home at the close of the day. When we set out the next day for several lectures I was to deliver, I discovered that I had left my wallet at our children's home, and there was no way to retrieve it until nighttime. My wife did the driving, and after the first lecture, we went to a restaurant for lunch. As we entered the restaurant I asked my wife whether she had any money, because I did not have my wallet. It turned out that she had only taken along her driver's license, and since we did not have money to pay for lunch, we returned to the car hungry.

We then began to think whether we had any acquaintances in the neighborhood where we could get a cup of coffee to hold us through the rest of the day. My wife remembered that a friend of hers, Debra, used to live in the neighborhood, but since she had not been in touch with her for seven years, she did not know whether she was still living here. We contacted "information" via our cellular phone, and Debra indeed still lived here, and a call to her resulted in a warm invitation.

Debra quickly whipped up a lunch, and the two friends chatted for an hour, renewing a beautiful friendship which had been neglected, and promising to stay in close touch hereafter.

Earlier in the day we had been very upset by the absence of a wallet, but just look at the benefits that resulted!

30.

WELL-CHOSEN WORDS

Several decades ago, books began appearing with guidelines on proper communication. A bit later, physiologists described the "type A" personality, an individual who upon being pressured by time considerations results in a number of inappropriate behaviors, one of which is interrupting others and finishing their sentences for them. They claim that "type A" personalities have a higher risk of coronary heart disease and high blood pressure.

Several thousand years ago, the sages of the Talmud defined proper communications:

There are seven characteristics of a wise person. He does not begin to speak before someone wiser than him; he does not interrupt the words of others; he does not answer impetuously; he asks relevant questions and he replies appropriately; he discusses first things first and last things last; he does not hesitate to admit he does not know something; and he acknowledges the truth (*Ethics of the Fathers* 5:9)

I doubt that any better guidelines to effective communication can be found anywhere. Interrupting others and finishing their sentences for them is annoying. I don't like when others do it to me, yet it has taken some effort for me to extend this courtesy to others. I have a high regard for people who allow me to finish what I have to say. Interrupting others shows you are impatient with them, and sets them on edge. Overcoming this particular manifestation of impatience may well lead to a general reduction of impatience. The physiologists are accurate in saying that this can lower the level of stress and prevent health problems that are stress related.

Each of the recommendations enumerated by the Talmud can help reduce stress. Listening to someone wiser may prevent one from making incorrect assumptions and foolish assertions. Impetuous answers are often wrong and provocative. Asking and responding relevantly and in an orderly fashion can avoid considerable confusion. Failure to admit that one is unaware of something and affecting knowledge of it may result in acting out of ignorance, which can be very damaging. Finally, events of the past several years have proven beyond the shadow of a doubt that trying to cover up mistakes or wrongdoing is both futile and destructive.

31.

DON'T RESPOND PREMATURELY, EVEN IN THOUGHT

In the preceding article, we noted the Talmudic guidelines on communication, among which are to not interrupt another's speech and to not answer impetuously. This is not restricted to verbal interruption and impetuosity, but to *mental* as well. Mental interruption and impetuosity occur when you begin *thinking* about a response before the other person has finished talking.

In halachah there is a rule that a judge may not listen to the argument of one litigant in the absence of the other. Rabbi Chaim Shmulevitz points out that if a judge hears one side, he is likely to be impressed with that litigant's position and may lose his objectivity. When the other litigant presents his argument, the judge may see it through colored glasses.

Much the same can happen when you begin thinking about your response before the other person has finished talking. He may go on to present other information that will shed a different light on the subject. If you do not wait to hear it before formulating your response, you may form an opinion which may be difficult to change. If you begin to think about your response before hearing all the facts, you have essentially assumed a position, and you may have unwittingly become biased. This is particularly true if what the other person has said has made you angry. Once anger sets in, objective judgment goes out the window. You become defensive about your position, and any information that might alter it may be dismissed.

It is difficult enough to hold your peace when you feel like interrupting. It is even more difficult to control your thoughts and not form an opinion until the other person has finished talking. It may help if you put yourself in his place. Would you like others to jump to conclusions before hearing everything you have to say?

I received a letter describing a case of severe spouse abuse, and as I read about the abusive behavior, I became very angry at the husband for his lack of consideration and irascible behavior. In the last paragraph, I discovered that the writer was the *husband*, describing how he was the victim of abuse by his wife. I had to reread the entire letter, because I had already formed an image of the husband as the villain, and that impression was not easily undone.

Be patient and be fair. Delay thinking about how you wish to respond until you have heard everything.

32.

SILENCE SPEAKS IN A LOUD VOICE

There is still more to say about effective communication. When you listen attentively to what the other person is saying, he is impressed with your interest and will take your response much more seriously. If you allow your thoughts to wander or start formulating your response while he is still talking, he will know you are not paying full attention to him, and he is likely to dismiss your response.

You might ask: How can the other person measure the degree of my attentiveness? He is not a mind reader, is he? No, one does not have to be a mind reader to gauge another person's attitude. We probably communicate more nonverbally than we do with words. For example, if the person you are talking to is doing something that requires concentration while you are talking, like continuing to write while ostensibly listening to you, you know that he cannot possibly be giving you full attention. Furthermore, you feel that his attitude is that whatever you have to say is not important. The same thing can happen when you stop listening and begin formulating your response, or if you allow your mind to wander away from the subject. You cannot conceal your attitude, because we do not have full control of our body language, and your stance will give it away.

The Torah tells us to love others as we do ourselves. Suppose that the other person is complimenting you about something you did. When you hear yourself being praised, your mind will *never* wander, and you will not only be fully attentive, but will also savor every single word. Similarly, if what he is telling you is what you want to hear, you will be most attentive. It is when the other person is speaking about himself or about something that is important to him that you tend to become a bit bored. Cultivating greater consideration for others will make what is important to them be important to you as well, and you will become a good listener. You will also discover how attentive the other person becomes to what you have to say, and this is an excellent way to foster good relationships.

33.

CONVERTING A MISTAKE INTO SOMETHING MEANINGFUL

You have heard it said, "If life gives you lemons, make lemonade!" That is good advice.

None of us are perfect. The only question is: Do we know what to do when we discover we have made a mistake? Of course, we should resolve never to repeat the mistake, and perhaps we may even be able to determine how and why we made that mistake, which should help us avoid repeating it. But then what?

A surgeon once ran into some serious complications during an operation, and asked the operating room nurse to see if there was anyone in the surgeon's lounge who could assist him. She said, "The chief of surgery is there. Should I call him?"

"Oh, no," the doctor said. "He's never gotten into a mess like this. He wouldn't know what to do." Being exceptionally skillful has its advantages, but may also have its drawbacks.

The Talmud is very clear about the proper attitude toward mistakes. "A person does not have a proper grasp of a halachah unless he errs in it" (*Gittin* 43a). Ironically, a rabbi who issued an incorrect judgment and had to correct it may have a better understanding of the law than someone who had it correct from the start! "The place occupied by a penitent cannot be attained by a perfectly righteous individual" (*Berachos* 34b).

Rabbi Levi Yitzchak of Berditchev once met a person who was a known sinner. "How I envy you!" the rabbi said.

"Envy me?" the man said. "Clearly, you jest."

"No. no," the rabbi said. "You see, the Talmud says that when a person does sincere repentence, all the sins he did are converted to merits. One day you will repent and you will have far more merits than me."

Obviously, one may not intentionally do wrong with the expectation that when he rectifies the wrong he will have merits. But if we discover that we have done wrong, and are sincere in correcting it and learning from the experience, we will have converted a liability into an asset.

The first reaction to discovering that one has made a mistake is and should be remorse. But after one has had remorse and has resolved not to let this happen again, one should look for ways in which the wisdom gained from the error can be put to good use. Then, instead of moping for days, one can turn one's attention in a positive direction.

34.

KEEP YOUR INTERESTS FRESH

If you have ever tried to put a child to sleep, you know how difficult that may be. The child will run out of bed, and find a hundred excuses to stay up. On the other hand, many adults can hardly wait until they can go to sleep. Why the stark difference?

Children are curious. The world is a relatively new place for them, and there are so many things to discover. Their curiosity is stimulating, and they want to learn ever more about the exciting world they are in. Adults often lose this stimulating curiosity. Everything is old hat, and the world becomes a boring place. Of course you will want to go to sleep when you are bored.

There is much in the world that is exciting. The fund of available knowledge is more than a person could absorb in several lifetimes. We now have at our disposal not only books but also audiotapes and videos that can put the world at our fingertips. We can learn about other cultures and about history. We can watch tapes about underwater life or the fascinating lives of animals in the jungle. The world is anything but boring!

Why then does a person become bored? Because he sees no practical application of this knowledge. How is my life going to be better if I learn about how bees communicate? Why, it is fascinating to learn how a bee that has found a food source returns to the hive, and by dancing in a particular way conveys to the other bees exactly where to find the food! Our interests should not be limited to only those things that will increase our assets or bring us greater comfort.

The Psalmist says, "How abundant are Your works, God! With wisdom You made them all" (*Psalms* 104:24). Maimonides says that a person can develop reverence of and love for God through the study of nature. Today, as never before, whether with the microscope that lets us enter the world of molecules or with the telescope that introduces us to the world of great galaxies, we can achieve an appreciation of the majesty of God.

One of the chassidic rabbis said that there are things we can learn from observing a small child. We can learn to always have a feeling of freshness, and be excited to learn more about the many wonders of the world. Then, like the child, our lives will not be boring.

35.

CRYING IS NOT A SIN (AND CERTAINLY NOT A SHAME)

Sometimes we read in the paper about an event so tragic that "some people cried unashamedly." I have great difficulty understanding this. Why should anyone be ashamed of crying?

Oh, yes. I have heard the expression, "He's nothing but a cry baby." But that refers to someone who whimpers over every little thing, which is indeed infantile. However, when misfortune strikes, why should a person be expected to hold back his tears?

Some people are hesitant to shed tears publicly, and other people are very uneasy when someone cries in their presence. When they do so, someone tries to change the subject, in an effort to distract the person from his pain.

I can remember when I was grieving, and I felt a need to talk and to cry. It was obvious to me that some people felt uncomfortable if I cried in their presence. In fact, I have noticed that some people may avoid a person who is in sorrow if they think he may cry. My solution was to go to A.A. meetings, because there the people were not afraid of emotions, neither to observe them, nor to share them.

Crying can be therapeutic and is a normal component of the grief process. If one shares his feelings with others and cries, it may be even more therapeutic than crying in solitude. If you happen to be in the presence of someone who is crying because of a loss, just sit by quietly. There is no need to say anything, certainly not, "There, there, don't cry now." You might reach over and gently hold the person's hand. Touch, too, can be therapeutic.

Let us not deprive someone of the healing that occurs in the grief process. If we feel uncomfortable because someone is crying in our presence, it may only mean that we are feeling his pain. That compassion is just what the person may need in order to heal.

36.

EXPECT THE BEST, NOT THE WORST

When I wish to relax, I lie back on an easy chair and let my mind drift back to when I was 10 years old, when we spent a few weeks in a bungalow near a lake. I can relive all the enjoyable activities of the day. What does a 10-year-old do all day in the country other than have fun?

One time I was at a spa, taking whirlpool treatments for my back. I was on vacation, away from all stress. After the whirlpool, I was in the "cooling-off" room, where I was lying quietly, wrapped in a sheet, totally free of any pressures. I did not have a phone to answer, letters to write, appointments to keep, etc. I could lie there comfortably and relax. Do you know what? I found myself drifting off again to Cedar Lake at age 10.

A bit later I reflected how foolish this was. Why did I have to imagine a scene from the past in order to relax, when I was in a state of maximum relaxation right now? In fact, sometime in the future when I wish to relax, I may well drift back to the scene in the "cooling-off" room, where I was free of all stress and pressures. Why couldn't I achieve maximum relaxation in the present, rather than have to go back to the past?

I gave this some thought, and I think I understand why. You see, when I thought about a day at Cedar Lake, that day had come to a close after having been a pleasant day. Nothing had happened later in that day to irritate me in any way. As for today, granted that at this moment, while lying in the "cooling-off" room my situation is very conducive to relaxation, but the day is not over yet. Any number of things may yet happen today that could upset me. That is why the relaxation of the past is superior to the relaxation of the present. I knew how the past ended, but I don't know how the present will end.

But isn't that rather foolish? Why should I anticipate something bad happening? Why shouldn't I be able to enjoy the present to the fullest? After all, we really live in the present. What is it with us that we are not at peace because of morbid expectations?

I am probably not unique in having anxiety about what may happen, and if you are like me, you may find the method I use to reduce this senseless stress helpful.

Every morning I recite Psalm 112 and say "He will not fear bad tidings, because his heart is firm with trust in God." This reassures me that as long as I believe that God is looking after me, I have nothing to fear. Even the things that appear to me as unpleasant are not harmful, because God is my protector. I then

90

say Psalm 121, "God will protect you from all evil … God will watch over your coming and your going, from now unto eternity."

I wish I could tell you that my faith in God is so complete that the present day becomes as secure as the day of the past which ended being thoroughly enjoyable. I'm not quite there yet, but it is certainly very reassuring to know that the fears I have are groundless.

37.

AMBITION OR PROVING YOURSELF?

Some people are ambitious. They are full of energy and have a need to expend it. They have much to offer and actually have a feeling of some kind of discomfort until they give of themselves, much like a nursing mother who is uncomfortable until the infant nurses. We can all remember having teachers who just loved to teach and to share their knowledge with their students. Both the nursing mother and the teacher repeatedly feel this need to give of themselves, and repeatedly do so. This is the nature of *ambitious* people.

There are other people who do much the same thing, but for an entirely different reason. These are people who have unwarranted feelings that they are inadequate and unworthy, and they are constantly doing things to prove, both to themselves and to others, that they are *not* inadequate or unworthy. They may be very productive and accomplish a great deal, but they are constantly under the stress of the feeling that they have not adequately proven themselves, and they are therefore in a constant state of unhappiness.

People who can be productive and accomplish much should indeed do so, but for the right reasons. They should be aware of their gifts and talents and wish to share them with others. They should feel good about themselves and be happy with their achievements, yet always desirous of doing still more. In other words, instead of *proving themselves*, they should become *ambitious*.

If you find yourself doing many things, such as being active in public service or giving much time to organizational work, pause and think for a moment. "Do I have a need to prove myself? Am I happy about what I have done?" If you are someone who repeatedly needs to prove yourself, you might try to do something about building up your self-esteem so that you can accomplish the same things and even more because you are ambitious. This will make you even more productive and much happier.

You might ask: How do I go about improving my self-esteem? Read on.

38.

MAYBE I DO HAVE AN ERRONEOUS SELF-CONCEPT

Some people ask me, "With your busy schedule, when did you find time to write 28 books?" I tell them that I never wrote 28 books. Rather, I wrote *one* book in 28 different ways.

That's true. Everything I wrote is in one way or another related to the theme that most peoples' problems in life are due to their having unwarranted feelings of inadequacy, or low self-esteem. You can find an expansion of this theme and many examples of how it plays out in everyday life in *Life's Too Short (St. Martin's Press)*, where you will also find some suggestions for overcoming low self-esteem.

One of the major difficulties is the inability of a person to accept that his self-image and his feelings of inferiority are indeed unwarranted. People who feel negative about themselves in one or more ways are absolutely certain that their self-perception is correct, and that they are indeed deficient.

Having proper self-esteem does not at all mean that a person should be vain and think that he is the greatest. It simply means not denying one's strengths, gifts and talents. The ethicist, Rabbi

Yehudah Leib Chasman, says, "Denying your God-given talents is not humility. It is stupidity."

Attaining good self-esteem must begin with the realization that, "Maybe I am really not what I have thought of myself. Maybe I do have an erroneous self-concept." Once you have this awareness, you are halfway there.

There are several fine books on self-esteem in the "self-help" and psychology section of your bookstore. Read them. Some of them have some self-esteem enhancing exercises, which can be helpful.

Organizing a small group of people who are interested in maximizing their potential is helpful. Finally, it is sometimes necessary to get some counseling from a therapist skilled in self-esteem problems.

It is really a shame for a person to suffer unnecessarily. Without exception, a better self-image results in added happiness and greater productivity.

39.

THEY ARE REALLY NOT TALKING ABOUT YOU

Sometimes you have an uncomfortable feeling that people are talking about you or that they are looking at you in a critical way. This is probably not true, and it does not mean that you're paranoid because you feel this way, although we must admit that it does have a touch of paranoia.

Having talked about the importance of self-esteem, let me point out something that may appear paradoxical. If you are under the impression that people are talking about you, stop and think a moment. What makes you think you are so important that others take cognizance of you and that they make you the subject of their conversation? They probably couldn't care less whether you're there or not. They have many more important things on their mind than to pay attention to you.

Wow! Isn't that a blow to self-esteem? Not at all. If you recall, self-esteem means having an awareness of your strengths and talents, and knowing that you can achieve and accomplish. It does not mean feeling "I am special" or "I am important," which are notions of vanity rather than feelings of self-esteem. In fact, it may be that the person who lacks self-esteem and feels that he is unworthy or inferior may try to protect himself from such feelings by thinking, "I am important," which may indeed result in his thinking that other people are concerned enough about him to make him the focus of their attention and conversation.

Suppose that just as you walk into a crowded room you see someone walking out. He is probably looking for a telephone, but if you are really insecure and have to elevate your self-esteem, you may think, "He's leaving the room because he saw me coming in." The other person probably didn't even notice you.

If you are okay with yourself, you won't worry that others may be talking about you. Develop a good self-esteem. You will be much more comfortable.

40.

POSITIVE PARENTING

Today's parents of young children may be legitimately concerned as to how they can protect their children from the epidemic use of alcohol and drugs among youth. While we do not have a fool-proof method of prevention, there are some things we can do to decrease the likelihood of our children being attracted to drugs.

The human being is comprised of three components : body, mind, and spirit. Mind refers to intellect, but even a person of high intellectual achievement may not necessarily be a spiritual person. The spirit is comprised of all the capacities which are unique to humans and are not found in other living things.

The human body is essentially an animal body with all the cravings that this implies. All our animalistic drives are geared toward gratification of the body's desires. They cannot be outward directed or altruistic. It has never happened that a tiger has said, "Let me give some of this carcass to that poor little jackal. He looks so hungry." The ability to give of oneself, in a gesture of loving kindness, is a uniquely human trait.

(A comprehensive discussion of spirituality can be found in *Twerski on Spirituality;* Shaar Press 1998.)

It is true that the human intellect is far superior to that of other living things, but intellect alone is not enough. A person may be very erudite and have many degrees, yet be thoroughly self-centered. What really distinguishes a human being from other forms of life is the ability of acting towards others with loving kindness, along with a number of other important traits, such as the capacity to improve oneself, the capacity to contemplate the purpose of existence, and the capacity to make free moral decisions. The common denominator of all the traits that define a human being is that they are not directed to self-gratification. When a person exercises the various capacities of the spirit, he is being spiritual.

Dedicated parents are diligent in providing the optimum in health care for their child, enabling him to have a healthy body. They are likely to avail him of the finest educational resources, to develop his intellect to the fullest. The same diligence is not always directed toward the third component: the spirit. Just as laxity in care of the mind and body may result in their being defective, so may laxity in the development of the spirit result in a defect.

A young person who is lacking in development of the spirit is likely to feel that he is somehow incomplete, but may not be able to identify what it is that causes him to feel that way. He is surrounded by an environment where recourse to chemicals, whether alcohol or drugs, is extremely common. Inasmuch as these substances are addictive, the danger of addiction is significant.

The more a youngster develops his spiritual traits, the less likely he is to fall victim to addiction. He develops a goal in life other than that of pleasure seeking, and may even be able to accept some discomforts in pursuit of an ultimate goal.

While observance of Torah that is limited to ritual practices does not forestall the self-destructive behaviors, the development of spirituality may indeed do so. It is not by coincidence that the popular and most effective programs for recovery from addiction emphasize spirituality, since a lack of spirituality renders one vulnerable to addiction.

The answer to the parents' question on how to try and prevent their children from falling prey to addiction is to provide at least as much for development of the spirit as for the body and mind. We must bear in mind, however, that didactic teaching is rather ineffective. Our children may not do what we say, but they are much more apt to do what they see us do. The most effective way of teaching spirituality to our children is to model for them, and by the way we live, show them how this is done.

41

WANT TO BE NUDNIK-PROOF?

One of the most difficult predicaments is to be at the mercy of a nudnik. This is a person who has little of substance to say, but takes forever to say it. He may hang on you as with suction cups, and short of being very abrupt and outspokenly rude, there seems to be no way to get rid of him. One such visit is enough to test one's patience. A supernudnik is one who comes back time after time. You may be a sensitive soul and you do not wish to hurt his feelings by telling him to stay away. What can you do?

If he visits you on a summer day, you may turn off the air-conditioning and when it gets hot, serve him a steaming glass of tea. This usually works, but is of no help in winter. You might excuse yourself, go upstairs, and call a friend with the request that they call you back in five minutes. The friend should shout loud enough over the phone so that it is audible across the room, and demand that you come over immediately because of an emergency.

Such tactics work for the nudnik. The supernudnik, however, keeps coming back. To keep your sanity, follow this simple suggestion. Size up his financial status. If he seems to have money, tell him you need a loan. He is not likely to come back so fast. If he doesn't have money, lend him some. To avoid paying back, he'll stay away.

These may be extreme tactics, but are justified in such desperate situations.

42.

YOU ARE WORTH IT

You're really unhappy about not being able to stop smoking, aren't you? Your wife has been persistently begging you to stop, and your only concession was that you no longer smoke in the house. The kids have been pleading with you to stop, and the fact is that you really would like to stop. You want to live longer and be healthier, and you are well aware of the many harmful effects of smoking. But each time you stop, the compulsion to pick up a cigarette is just too overwhelming.

Every little bit of help in winning this battle is welcome. So let's look at it this way.

Suppose you are fortunate in having a new luxury automobile, say, a shiny new Porsche. How careful you would be that it not get dented or even scratched! No doubt you would make sure that it is frequently waxed to protect the surface and maintain its luster. The reason for your meticulous care of the car is because you see and know it to be valuable and beautiful. There is a natural instinct to protect something that is valuable and beautiful from being damaged.

Now, if you only felt yourself to be valuable and beautiful, you would have a strong resistance to doing anything that threatened to damage you, and that would include smoking. If only your self-perception was correct, you would have a powerful ally in your battle against the compulsion to smoke.

You may say, "There you go again with your preoccupation with self-esteem." Indeed so, but the logic is infallible. You might not exert much caution about your earthenware coffee mug, but you are very careful about your fine crystal stemware. The latter never go into the dishwasher, and are washed and dried carefully by hand, then placed in the china cupboard in a way that they should not be damaged.

When your self-esteem improves, everything becomes better, and you will find the ability to stop smoking much easier to achieve.

43

DON'T WAIT FOR THE OTHER PERSON TO SAY HE'S SORRY

O.K., so you've had a disagreement with someone, maybe an argument in which both of you said some uncomplimentary things, and now you are angry at each other. After some time passes, you regret having offended him, but your pride does not let you apologize. After all, the other person also made some nasty remarks, maybe even worse than yours. Let him apologize first.

Unfortunately, the other person may be feeling exactly the same way, and if you both cling to your pride and stand on ceremony, a friendly relationship may be doomed forever. Furthermore, once we develop a negative or hostile attitude, it is not unusual for us to justify our feelings, so we begin to look for more reasons why we should dislike that person, and before you know it, a few foolish comments may make friends hate one another. There is more than enough hatred in the world, and we certainly do not need to add to it.

The Talmud tells us that when the High Priest, Aaron, heard of two people who had become estranged, he would say to one of them, "You know, your friend really feels badly about what he said to you. He desperately wants to preserve the friendship, but he is so ashamed of what he said that he just can't muster the courage to approach you to apologize. Next time you meet him, don't keep your distance, It will make it easier for him to apologize." Then Aaron would go to the other party and tell him exactly the same thing. The next time the two met, each was convinced that the other wished to apologize but could not assert himself, and they would try to facilitate the apology for the other person. In no time, they would be friends again.

Aaron did not lie. The fact is that people invariably regret having made insulting or hostile remarks in the heat of a dispute, and it is a false pride that thwarts their desire to set things straight. If only something could remove this barrier and give them a face-saving way to apologize, they would gladly do so. Aaron interpreted people's feelings correctly, and merely provided the face-saving maneuver for each.

Unfortunately, there are not too many "Aarons" around to remove the barriers to reconciliation, and false pride results in unnecessary escalation of hard feelings between friends. So be your own "Aaron," and assume that the other person truly regrets having said some foolish things. Be honest with yourself, won't you? Take the initiative in stretching out the olive branch. You will be richly rewarded.

44.

HEAR NO EVIL, SPEAK NO EVIL

You know what it feels like when you're with a small group of people, and someone relates a piece of juicy gossip about someone else, whether an acquaintance, a prominent person in the community, or a government official. There is some kind of enjoyable feeling listening to this, isn't there? Or when you know something about someone else, and just can't wait until you have the opportunity to tell this to someone. Even the anticipation is pleasant, let alone the actual telling.

Have you ever wondered what makes gossip enjoyable? A delicacy is pleasant to the taste buds, fine music is pleasing to hear, and drama stimulates one's interest. But what is there about hearing or speaking of another person's shortcomings that makes it so delectable?

There is a proverb, "What makes a small child happy? Seeing a child that is smaller than himself." A small child feels dwarfed by the giant adults around him, and this may give him a feeling of insignificance. We often see a child climbing on a chair and declaring, "Look how big I am," and this leaves no doubt how he feels about his diminutive size. When this child sees that he is bigger than someone else, this elevates his status. He is not the tiniest person in the world after all.

Grownups who have feelings of inferiority are no different from the small child. If they feel that everyone around them is more intelligent, more wealthy, better looking, and/or more skillful than they are, this may cause them great discomfort. If they can feel that others are deficient in any way, this can give them a feeling of being superior to them, or at least, less inferior.

This, then, is why disparaging others is so pleasant. It provides a much needed uplift for a fragile ego. If someone speaks badly about another person, you know that he must feel inadequate and unworthy, and, that others' defects are a balm to his distressed ego. If you enjoy listening to him, this indicates that you, too, are in need of such an artificial ego support, let alone if you are the one who is doing the talking.

Try to overcome your feelings of inferiority, for then you won't have to betray how you feel about yourself by listening to or speaking about another person's shortcomings.

45

GROWTH IS NOT PAINLESS

H uman beings should not be stagnant. Animals can grow only in mass, and when they reach their maximum size, there is no further growth. People, however, have a spiritual component which can continue to grow long after physical growth has come to an end.

Spiritual growth and self-improvement invariably require our making some changes in our behavior, and these changes are rarely easy. Some changes constitute major challenges, and we may be frightened off by the discomfort in instituting them. Here is where the story about lobsters is helpful.

Have you ever thought about how a lobster can grow, since it is confined within a rigid shell? The answer is that when a lobster grows inside its shell, it eventually feels confined and compressed, and the discomfort causes it to shed its shell and grow a new and more spacious one. This process is repeated until the lobster reaches its maximum size. Although the shedding of the shell may be accomplished in the crevices of underwater rocks, the naked lobster is nevertheless vulnerable to being eaten by a predatory fish. In other words, the lobster must risk its life in order to grow.

The stimulus for the lobster to shed its confining shell and to grow is the feeling of discomfort at being compressed. This is also true of human beings for whom, too, the feeling of uneasiness may be nature's way of telling them, "It's time for you to grow."

Unfortunately, many people do not interpret this signal correctly, and instead of making the necessary effort to grow, they try to find some way to relieve their discomfort. Some turn to alcohol, others to tranquilizers, and yet others to some escapist technique. The tragedy is that they ignore or suppress the stimulus for growth.

As noted, growth may require some changes that are difficult to make. But remember, the lobster has to risk its very life in order to grow. People do not have to jeopardize their very lives, but must learn to tolerate the discomfort involved in growth.

46.

NOT EVERYTHING EMOTIONAL
IS PSYCHOLOGICAL

In 1960 I began my psychiatric training, at which time the prevailing theory was that a person's feelings and reactions are primarily if not entirely due to psychological factors in his past or to various circumstances in the present. This made perfectly good sense, and I believed it.

In 1962 I became depressed, and I knew exactly why this had happened. On a meager resident's salary, I had bought a house and assumed a large mortgage. Furthermore, I was piqued by the way I was being treated by some family members. There were also several other irritating things that I felt were the cause of my depression.

I was very reluctant to disclose my condition to any of my psychiatric instructors, for fear that they would dismiss me from the training program. Who needs a psychiatrist with emotional problems of his own? But when the depression increased in severity, I had no choice.

After listening to my tale of woe, my professor asked, "Abe, are you taking any medication?" "Only something for hay fever," I said, and I told him the name of the medication. "Why don't you stop the medication for awhile, and let's see what happens," he said. I had no idea what he was talking about, because my problem was that I was depressed because of all these stresses.

However, I stopped taking the pill, and after several days the depression began to lift. By the end of two weeks I was back to my cheerful self. One of the possible side effects of this medication is that it can result in depression, and that is what had happened to me.

The important thing to note is that before and after I took the medication, I had the same mortgage and was subject to the same family relationships, and all of the other irritants were also present. My past history had *not* changed one iota. My depression had obviously *not* been the result of either psychological causes in the past or even the stresses of the present, but totally due to a side effect of a medication. Had you asked me during the depressive phase why I was feeling that way, I would have given you the causes which I believed to be responsible for my depression, none of which were true.

The point of this story is that if you have days when you feel that everything in your life is going wrong, don't believe it for a minute. As with me, both your past and present circumstances were little different several days ago, yet you were not feeling down then.

Don't jump to the wrong conclusions when you're in a bad

mood. You may create problems where none exist in reality. Give yourself a little time to get over the mood, and you'll discover that what you thought were the problems causing your mood really had nothing at all to do with it.

47.

NOW, ISN'T THAT ABSURD?

Sometimes when you are bothered by something, you may feel better if you consciously exaggerate the irritant to the point of absurdity.

You may feel stupid because you forgot to turn off the stove before you left home, and not only is the stew burnt to a crisp, but the pot will take days to scrub clean. You berate yourself for your negligence. Now is a good time to think, "Yes, and on the evening news, CNN will broadcast to the entire world that Judith burned the dinner and ruined the pot. All the parliaments in the world will interrupt what they are doing and take up the problem of Judith's stew and her pot. Everyone on the street will be talking about it, and if I go shopping downtown, everybody will be saying, 'Look, there goes Judith! She's the one who burned the stew and ruined the pot.'" Before long you'll be laughing at yourself.

I recall a woman who was referred to me because she had undergone radiation treatment for a lesion on her nose. There was a blemish on her nose which would eventually heal completely, but she was beside herself with anxiety about how ugly this made her look. Her husband and her doctor had tried to reassure her, but she was inconsolable.

I saw no reason to believe that my reassurances would be any more effective. Instead I said, " Oh, I knew about that, Becky. I was listening to the dialogue between the astronauts in orbit and the control center, and I heard the astronauts say, 'We've got our cameras and telescope focused on Becky's nose, and we can see that red spot from way up here. In fact, it is so bright that it obscures the sun. How can the country continue to function when Becky's nose looks so terrible? Are you sure that we will be safe up here and that the people at the space center will not be distracted by Becky's nose?' I knew it would be only a matter of time before you would come to me with this horrendous problem that is upsetting the entire world."

In spite of herself, Becky began to laugh. "You're making fun of me," she said. "No, I am not," I said. "You are the one that is making fun of yourself by making that tiny little spot the focus of your life. No one else notices it or cares about it." Becky agreed, and the situation was defused.

Very often, things bother us because we blow them out of proportion. If shrinking them down to size doesn't work, try the opposite. Exaggerate them to the point of absurdity, and you may be able to see how relatively trivial they really are.

48.

COPING WITH PAIN

Pain is *not* small stuff.

I know whence I speak. I am writing this as I sit in the dentist's office waiting impatiently for him to call me in so that he can do something about this terrible toothache. It began to hurt this morning, and I am very grateful that he could see me as an emergency.

Pain shrinks the world. As far as I am concerned now, nothing exists except this tooth which is causing me excruciating, throbbing pain, all the way behind my eyes. I am not interested in anything else at this moment except for relief. I don't even want to know *why* it is hurting. I just want the pain to stop. If someone told me that a hundred astronauts had just landed on Mars and were sending back pictures of an ancient civilization, I would not be in the least interested. As distressing as this pain is, it is nevertheless allowing me to write. I am not completely dysfunctional. Do you know why? Because I know that in a short while I will feel better, and that knowledge enables me to be sufficiently tolerant of the pain to write. Acute pain, as severe as it may be, can be weathered.

Chronic pain is something totally different. Pain that lingers on and on can be totally disruptive, especially if there is no treatment that can eliminate the cause of the pain. If there is no light at the end of the tunnel, chronic pain can render a person dysfunctional. In desperation, people often turn to potent pain-killing medication for relief. While this is perfectly understandable, the fact is that if these medications are of the addictive type, they may lose their effectiveness effect after a while. The person will then take a larger dose to avoid suffering. This larger dose is also likely to become ineffective, and as the pattern continues, the person may develop a serious addiction. The end result of this is that the very large doses of pain-killers can result in confusion and emotional symptoms, *yet the pain persists* .

What can one do for relief from chronic pain? First of all, consult a clinic that specializes in chronic pain, because there are some methods of pain relief that do not involve habituating drugs. To this one must add an attitudinal approach. It is important to remain active, both occupationally and socially in spite of the pain. *Don't let your body push you around!* If you let the pain restrict your functioning, it may be extremely hard to get out of the rut.

When there is no total relief from pain, some people get angry at God for being afflicted. "Why me?" they say. There is no satisfactory answer to this question. On the other hand, there is much in Torah literature on accepting suffering, how to cope with distress that cannot be relieved. These concepts were written by spiritual people who suffered agonizing pain, yet instead of being angry with God, they were able to turn their suffering into a spiritual growth experience. Together with whatever relief can be safely provided, an upbeat attitude can actually decrease the suffering.

In contrast to acute pain, where the patient is the only one that needs to be involved by taking the medication, chronic pain requires an adjustment by the family as well as the patient. An understanding and supportive family who, together with the patient, receive counseling, can go a long way in alleviating the misery.

49.

THERE IS A MASTER PLAN

I don't like to preach acceptance, because I'm not that good at it myself. Yet, in my work with people recovering from severe addictions, I see them regularly praying for God to give them the peace of mind that will enable them to have the patience for those things they cannot change. Some consider this the backbone of recovery, because if one cannot accept the inevitable "downs" of life with serenity, one is sure to react in some destructive way, whether it is drinking or something else.

I have always been impressed with the dramatic Biblical story of Joseph, how his jealous brothers sold him into slavery, then dipped his coat into goat's blood and led their father to believe that Joseph had been killed by a wild beast. Jacob grieved bitterly over the loss of his favorite child, who eventually rose to become viceroy of Egypt, and then revealed his identity to his brothers, saying, ""I do not hold a grudge against you. It was not you who sold me into slavery. God engineered all of this, and you were merely His agents, carrying out His design."

What was Jacob's reaction when he found out that his sons had sold their brother into slavery, and led him to believe he was killed, causing him to agonize with grief for twenty-two years? Since Jacob blessed his sons prior to his death, it is clear that he had forgiven them and loved them in spite of their atrocity. This could only be because Jacob agreed with Joseph's explanation, that the brothers were but God's instruments to carry out His plan to make Joseph viceroy of the mightiest empire in the world.

But of course, Jacob was the Patriarch, and we can hardly aspire to his spirituality. Nevertheless, we should have some degree of trust in G-d, and realize that although we may not be able to comprehend why He allows some terrible things to happen, there is a Divine plan. The world is really not haphazard and chaotic as it may seem.

I know that acceptance is not easy. If it was easy, there would not be any need for us to pray for the strength to accept adversity. But although acceptance is difficult, the trust that there is a purpose to everything makes it possible for us to survive.

50.

ACCENTUATE THE POSITIVES

T he chassidic rabbis said, "If it is defects you are looking for, try to find your own. If you wish to praise someone, direct your praises toward God." In other words, don't focus on other people's characters, especially not in order to find their faults.

The reason they discouraged indulging in someone's praises is because the Talmud states that when you say something complimentary about a person, someone is apt to remark, "Yes, but did you know that he..." and then proceed to say something uncomplimentary about him.

However, that is in regard to speaking about another person, in which case we are better off simply not to speak about him at all, so as not to give rise to the possibility of any negative comments being made. But as far as we ourselves are concerned, we should seek to find the virtues of other people and try to ignore any negative features they may have.

There is a beautiful prayer composed by Rabbi Elimelech of Lizhensk, which is to be recited before the morning service. In this prayer he says, "May we see the virtues of others and not their faults." This is a wonderful preparation for the morning prayer, and if we succeed in doing so, we may then invoke the principle that God relates to us the way we relate to others. In other words, God will then focus on *our* virtues and look away from our sins.

Just think what a wonderful world it would be if everyone observed only the good in other people, and, insofar as character defects are concerned, focused rather on their own. Perhaps we cannot convert the entire world to think this way, but we can do so ourselves. As we do so, others may emulate us, and we may serve as role models for our children.

So, as far as others are concerned, let us accentuate the positives and eliminate the negatives.

51.

YOU CAN EXPECT ONLY WHAT
YOU ARE

We often wish to tell others what they should do, and we certainly want to instruct our children how to act. Let us remember that we cannot expect of others to do more than we ourselves do.

The Psalmist says, "God has given His laws and His ordinances to Israel" (*Psalms* 147:19), upon which the commentators observe, "God has given us *His own* laws; i.e., the laws by which God Himself abides." God obeys His own laws.

Some people expect more of others than they do of themselves, and parents may also expect greater perfection from their children than they do of themselves. This is generally futile.

It is related that a couple had a son who indulged excessively in sweets. They were desperate for him to stop, because they felt it was detrimental to his health. Inasmuch as the young boy had a deep interest in Mahatma Gandhi, they decided to take the boy to Gandhi so that he could exercise his authority and prevail upon the boy to stop eating sweets.

After much time and great expense, they reached Gandhi and told him of their plight. Gandhi told them to come back in two weeks. They pleaded with Gandhi, telling him of the inordinate expense it would mean for them to stay away from their work for two weeks, but Gandhi was unyielding.

After two weeks they returned to Gandhi, who embraced the young boy and said gently but firmly, "Son, you must stop eating sugar and candy."

The bewildered parents asked Gandhi, "Why did you make us wait two weeks at such great cost to us? You could have said that two weeks ago."

Gandhi shook his head. "No," he said. "You see, two weeks ago *I myself* was eating sugar and sweets, hence I could not tell the boy not to do so."

The message is clear. Do not ask someone to do something which you are not doing yourself.

52.

YOU CAN'T OR YOU WON'T?

Rabbi Zusia was once hurrying along the way when someone called to him, "Hey there! Help me load these bales of hay on my wagon." Rabbi Zusia, who was late for an appointment, responded, "Sorry, but I can't." The man shouted back to him, "Yes you can! You just don't want to." Rabbi Zusia took this as an admonition from heaven that there are many things he does not do because he thinks he cannot do them, whereas the truth is that he just does not want to.

Inside our heads, there is an ingenious mechanism, a high-powered brain which seeks to protect our comfort. It can conjure up any rationalizations, so that when we do not *want* to do something, we convince ourselves that we *can't* do it, and this spares us from the guilt feeling which we would have if we were to think that we just don't want to do it.

The aphorism, "Where there is a will there is a way," is for the greater part true. Like many other generalizations, there are some exceptions to this rule. There are some things that are in fact beyond one's capability. In my office, I had a poster showing birds in flight with the caption "They fly because they think they can." If someone were to hypnotize me and give me the suggestion which I internalized that I could fly, it would not enable me to flap my wings and soar into the air. But with a few exceptions, the rule is valid. You do what you believe you can do.

So next time you resign yourself to not being able to do something, take a second look and try to be sincere. Is it really that you *cannot* do it, or that you would *rather* not do it? You may have valid reason for not wanting to do it, and if so, be truthful with yourself. This will help you avoid self-deception, and you will discover that there are more things that you can indeed do.

53.

ESCAPING REALITY

A number of years ago there was a commercial on the radio which was repeated numerous times, and I am sure that this repetition must have impacted on some people. Here is how the commercial went:

First woman: "Oh, Grace, what am I to do? My husband is bringing his boss home for dinner tonight and my sink drain is all clogged up. I'm so upset!"

Second woman: "There, there. Don't let yourself be upset. Just take some _____ _____ (brand name of tranquilizer)."

How foolish! If Grace had used good judgment, she would have suggested getting a plunger and/or a can of the drain-opening chemical and that would solve the problem. If push comes to shove, one could call a plumber. But taking a tranquilizer will *not* open the drain, and will only make the woman oblivious to the problem. Indeed, if she becomes so tranquilized that she tries to prepare the dinner in spite of a clogged-up sink drain, she will soon have a flooded kitchen, which will constitute an even worse problem.

In a lecture to the clients at our rehabilitation center, I cited this commercial as typical of addiction. Instead of coping with a reality problem, the addict takes a chemical to forget it.

Several months later I received a letter from a young woman who had been treated at our center for alcoholism and had attended that lecture. She said that she had wanted to show off her recovery by having a dinner at her home, to which she invited 15 people. The day of the dinner her sink drain was clogged up, and after working on it for two hours, her husband could not get it open. He was terrified about how his wife would react, knowing her history of recourse to alcohol.

The wife burst into laughter, which her husband could not understand. She used the powder-room sink to wash the vegetables, and after the dinner was over, she asked the guests to help carry the dishes down to the laundry sink in the basement. "They not only carried the dishes down, they even helped me wash them! I hate to think what I would have done if I would have still been drinking at the time."

Medication is for emotional illnesses, not for escaping reality. Using chemicals to escape from problems instead of coping with them will only complicate things. When you are confronted with a reality problem, try to resolve it. If you can't do it alone, get appropriate help. You are certain to be much happier.

54.

DON'T SPREAD MISERY

As I've indicated earlier, it is true that "a sorrow shared is halved," or if it's not halved, it is at least somewhat mitigated. But it is not always necessary to involve others in your distress. Sometimes it is better to spare others from misery, especially if there is nothing that they can do to help.

For example, you arrive at an important meeting, open your attaché case to take out the relevant documents, only to discover that they are not there! You distinctly recall taking them out in order to put into your attaché case at home, but obviously you must have left them on the desk. There is no one there who can fax them to you, and it would be rather difficult to fax almost 200 pages, anyway.

You apologize to everyone at the meeting, and you do your best to operate from memory, which is not too good. You promise to send them all the material when you get home. You castigate yourself for being so negligent as not to check your attaché case before you left. In the evening you call your wife. "How did everything go today, honey?" she asks. Should you tell her, "Absolutely terrible!" and recount the forgetting of the documents? This will certainly upset her, but will it make you feel any better?

If you truly feel that by sharing this episode with your wife you will be relieved somewhat, then go ahead. Husbands and wives are supposed to help each other in every possible way, even at some discomfort to themselves. But if telling her is not going to provide you with any benefit, why make your wife miserable for no good reason?

It is no different with friends. You find out that a mutual acquaintance has suffered a tragedy. Should you tell your friend about it? If doing so will enable him to be supportive to the sufferer in any way, as for example, to pay a condolence call or send a sympathy card, then by all means you should do so. But if it happens to be a situation where your friend can do nothing, what is gained by making him feel distressed about his friend's plight?

We have to exercise good judgment as to when to share bad tidings with others. When this is of no constructive use, a statement found in *Proverbs,* "One who delivers bad tidings is a fool," applies. It is only when some good can come of your sharing such information with others that you should do so.

55.

SOME MOUNTAINS MELT INTO MOLEHILLS

It is now 3 A.M. as I write this, and I have just returned from my grandson's wedding. It was a beautiful wedding.

I thought back to the groom's father's Bar Mitzvah 32 years earlier. We were having many guests for the Sabbath meal, and we prepared an exorbitant amount of gefilte fish which, because we did not have enough refrigerator space at home, we stored in the synagogue refrigerator. I was supposed to bring the fish home Friday afternoon.

When we returned from services Friday night, my wife asked for the gefilte fish. A chill went up and down my spine, and I felt frozen with paralysis, something characteristic of the worst anxiety attack possible. I had forgotten to bring home the fish! There was no way to bring the fish home as Orthodox Jews do not carry outdoors on the Sabbath. How does one start a Friday-night meal, especially the Bar Mitzvah feast, without gefilte fish? What would the guests think? Oh, my! How could this have happened?

Well, there was nothing more we could do about it. When the guests were all seated, I simply told the truth. They all laughed heartily, but I was not laughing at all. I had made the boo-boo of my lifetime, and I couldn't shake the feeling of embarrassment during the entire Bar Mitzvah weekend.

Tonight, when I looked at my son escorting his son to be wed — truly, one of my dreams coming true—believe me, the missing gefilte fish was of no consequence at all.

If you are eating your heart out about something similar to the calamity of the gefilte fish, why don't you just think about the fact that some day this is going to be so insignificant that it will hardly be worthwhile remembering? Let it begin to be insignificant now.

56.

AN IMAGE REFLECTED IN
THE WATER

I am at the airport at this moment, and I am writing this while the impression on my mind is still fresh.

I was on the moving walkway, and a gentleman who was standing next to me noticed someone he knew on the walkway going in the opposite direction. He began a conversation with her, but they were near each other only momentarily. Inasmuch as the walkways were going in opposite directions, the distance between them increased rapidly. They tried to carry on a conversation, but after a few seconds, they were too far apart to communicate.

This caused me to reflect. I would not be surprised if this is the reason for poor communication between spouses. The people on the walkways knew why their communication was getting progressively weaker. They could see that they were heading in opposite directions. In a marriage, however, the difference in goals between husband and wife may be much more subtle. The two may actually have different goals in life, and may essentially be heading in disparate directions. However, in contrast to the people in the walkway, they may not be aware of this. As the distance between them increases, their communication progressively deteriorates.

When a couple realizes that they're having problems communicating, the first thing they should do is to try and clarify what they each want out of life. If their goals are disparate, perhaps they can reconsider and bring their goals closer together.

Closeness and distance may have a profound impact on a relationship. In our morning prayers, we describe God's intense love for us. We then recite the portion of the Torah which instructs us that we should develop love for God. Someone pointed out that Solomon says, "Just as water reflects a person's image, so the feelings of one person toward another are a reflection of the latter's feelings for him" (*Proverbs* 29:19). Inasmuch as God loves us intensely, why is our love for Him not correspondingly intense?

The answer is that Solomon refers to a reflection in *water*, not in a mirror, and there is a great difference. A mirror will reflect an image from a distance, but water will reflect an image only if one is close to it. If we draw ourselves closer to God by doing His will, our love for Him will indeed increase, approaching His love for us.

The same holds true in a marriage. If there is too great a distance between the couple, the feelings for each other may become incongruous. If they find their goals to be divergent, perhaps they can modify them so that they are not heading in different directions. This will certainly improve their relationship.

138

57.

I'M NOT PERFECT, YOU'RE NOT PERFECT

We all know people who are perfectionists. Indeed, some degree of perfectionism is desirable. When I board an airplane, I hope that the pilot is sufficiently perfectionistic to carefully check all the dials and gauges in the cockpit. It is only when perfectionism gets out of hand that it causes trouble. If the pilot is not satisfied after thoroughly checking everything, and repeats his checking numerous times, the plane may never get to its destination in time.

One of the reasons for excessive perfectionism may be that a person may be very fearful of being criticized for making a mistake. Constructive criticism may be very helpful in showing us a way to improve ourselves, as Solomon states, "Criticize a wise person and he will love you"(*Proverbs* 9:8). As far as making a mistake is concerned, we should remember that all humans are fallible. *Ecclesiastes* (7:20) states that there is no righteous person on earth who does only good and never sins.

From what I have said earlier, you should be able to surmise what comes next. Yes, perfectionism and fear of criticism are indicative of low self-esteem. A person who feels competent and worthy may not like making a mistake, but his ego is strong enough to withstand the awareness that he has done so, and when this is called to his attention he is not devastated. To the contrary, he is appreciative that this was noted so that he can take the necessary steps to avoid repeating the mistake. A person who has a low opinion of himself may be terrified of being criticized, even if it is constructive criticism. He may therefore try to be perfect in order to avoid such an ego-shattering experience. Unfortunately, excessive perfectionism often results in poorer rather than better performance.

We should always try to do our best, but we should not be so terrified of criticism that we go to unreasonable extremes in order to avoid it. This is self-defeating. Learning from mistakes is a positive experience, and is not something which we should fear.

56.

TUNE IN

The soothing effect of music was well known in the times of the Prophets (*I Samuel* 16:23). In the fifth of his Eight Chapters, Maimonides strongly recommends music for relief of a dejected mood.

Many of us can attest to this. I once traveled over an hour through harrowing, construction-punctuated traffic to get to a meeting. When I discovered that the meeting had been postponed for three weeks and that I was not notified of this, I was fit to be tied. Not only did I waste precious time, but I also was faced with repeating the traffic ordeal. When I got back into the car I was tense, stressed out, and fuming.

I put on a cassette of my favorite classical music, and within minutes my tension began to melt like butter on a hot pan. I was actually not aggravated by the orange barrels and shifting lanes. I wished I had thought of the music earlier.

In addition to a soothing effect, music can also have a mood-elevating effect. Try this. Lock the door to your room, put on a tape or CD of lively, wedding-type music, and *start dancing*. You will be surprised how different you will feel. Of course, you should draw the blinds shut because someone might see you dancing around your office in midday. Not knowing that you are doing this for therapeutic purposes, they may think your behavior a bit strange.

"But," you might say, "I just don't feel like dancing." That's when you need it the most. Push yourself to dance. If it doesn't work, your money will gladly be refunded.

59.

THE JOY IN GRATITUDE

I f there is anything that characterizes human behavior, it is the pursuit of happiness. The founding fathers wisely listed this as "an inalienable human right." Unfortunately, many people may desperately grope for happiness in every which way, even turning to the euphoria of drugs to try and find it, which paradoxically results in nothing but misery.

There is true happiness in gratitude. I happen to be in an enviable position of providing treatment to people suffering from addictive conditions, and I frequently receive thank-you letters, the theme of which is, "I am now back with my family and back at my job. I never thought life could be this good." Or, "I have just graduated from nursing (law, medical, business) school, and I am embarking on a career which I had thought was beyond my reach." These letter close with, "I want to thank you for giving me back my life."

I can assure you that I get a "high" from these letters. This made me think whether I express my gratitude sufficiently to people who have done things for me. If we will only pay attention, there are many things people do for us that we may take for granted. I now dash off a brief thank-you note to people who have done something for me. I discovered that not only is there joy in *receiving* expressions of gratitude, but also in extending them. In addition, the knowledge that you are giving another person a good feeling is uplifting.

I now have a better understanding of the verses (*Psalms* 100:1-2), "A song of gratitude...serve God with joy." Yes, by expressing gratitude we can feel joy.

Just as light and darkness cannot coexist, and even a small light can banish much darkness, so can dejection and joy not coexist, and even a small amount of joy can help overcome dejection. So, if you happen to feel down, try to think of something that someone has done for you, and write a brief thank-you note to that person. You will see how much better this makes you feel. Best of all, this is an antidepressant that you can get at no cost and which has no undesirable side effects.

60.

I'VE GOT A LITTLE LIST

I t has been said that the pen is mightier than the sword. This refers to the ability of the written word to influence others. There is also much that writing can do for oneself.

If you are like me, you may go to the supermarket to purchase five items, which should be easy enough to remember. Quite often, once inside the store, you will remember only four of the five. If it were four items you wanted, you will remember only three. Don't ask why this happens. It just does. The best solution is to keep a pad of notepaper handy, and whenever you think about something you need, jot it down.

It is very likely that over the weekend you may think of several calls you wish to make on Monday. Write them down. As important as they may be, you are likely to forget one or more.

In treating alcoholics, I have become impressed with the benefits of making lists. The recovering alcoholic is required to do a careful soul-searching and make a list of his character defects. He can then work on correcting them. This is a particularly important list to make. We are very prone to be oblivious to some of our character defects.

The alcoholic is also required to make a list of all the people whom he had harmed as a result of his drinking. He must try to make amends to them. Again, since this may arouse unpleasant memories, these things are likely to escape one's attention unless one writes them down.

Alcoholics are not the only people with character defects that could stand correction, nor are they the only people who may have offended others. We are all vulnerable to these. We would be wise to periodically do some serious soul-searching and make a list of our character defects as well as of people to whom we should apologize.

By the way, if you can't think of anything to write down on your list of character defects, that may be the greatest defect of all. None of us are perfect, and if we are unaware of our imperfections, we will never be able to correct them. Character defects are apt to give rise to unhealthy actions, and improving upon them can eliminate many difficulties.

So, make lists. You'll be happier for it.

61.

KEEPING IT SIMPLE

Solomon sized up the world's problems in one sentence: "God created man simple, but they sought many intrigues" (*Ecclesiasties* 7:29). If people would stop complicating things, many problems could be solved. But no, man has a penchant for taking simple things and twisting them around.

A disciple once told the Rabbi of Rizhin that he was not sufficiently learned to know what was right and what was wrong, and he asked whether the Rabbi could give him some simple guidelines. The Rabbi responded, "Think of yourself as a tightrope walker. When a tightrope walker feels he is being tugged to one side, he maintains his balance by leaning a bit to the other side. Most of a person's drives are his biological impulses, which seek to be gratified. If you find yourself being attracted to do something, pause and lean a bit toward not doing it. That way you will maintain an even balance."

Like the disciple, we may often be uncertain whether a given action is right or wrong. Here is another good guideline: Is there a possibility that you might ever have to deny doing it? If yes, then don't do it! Another good rule: Will you have to make excuses for what you've done? If so, don't do it! We don't make excuses for having done what is right and we don't have to deny doing it. And yet another: Do you have to look around to see whether anyone is overhearing what you are about to say or whether anyone may be watching what you are doing? If so, don't say it and don't do it.

Just think of what life would be like if we adhered to these simple rules!

62.

OUR ROLES MAY CHANGE, BUT NOT OUR VALUE

Y ou've heard of the "empty nest syndrome." Children grow up and go off to study. They marry and move to another city. The house is empty. Mothers seem to be affected more than fathers, probably because the mother is often more intimately involved with the care of the child, whereas the father is at work all day.

At any rate, mothers may get depressed when the house empties out. There is nothing much to do in the house anymore. Most of the beds are not slept in. There is very little laundry. Cooking for two takes little time, and the couple often eat out. Why mess up the kitchen?

"Empty nest syndrome" mothers become depressed because they don't feel useful any more. This is where they are making a great mistake. Parents are *always* useful. It is just the nature of their function that changes.

When the child is a tiny infant, he needs constant attention: feeding, bathing, diapering, carrying, and looking after him when he is ill. As he grows older, he can dress and bathe himself. His mother still has to do his laundry, prepare his lunch, cook dinner, and clean his room. Some of this activity continues at intervals when he is off to school. His father may feel needed because he is helping out financially. But when the child marries and moves away and becomes financially self-sufficient, that's when parents may feel that they are no longer functional.

How wrong, how terribly wrong! I lived six hundred miles from my parents. I was established in my practice, and my parents did not have to *do* anything for me. But when the baby got his first tooth or took his first steps, I called and shared these great events with them. I sent them pictures of the children, and they called to tell me that these were unquestionably the most beautiful children in the world. When the children said something cute, my parents told me that my children were the brightest in the world. They came to the Bar Mitzvahs and graduations. There is abundant joy in raising a family when one can share good news with parents. And of course, one can receive comfort when things do not go well.

One of the saddest moments in my life was when I could no longer call my father or mother to share the pleasure of my children's progress. Sure, I received many congratulatory wishes from good friends, but a parent's good wishes are irreplaceable. I do take great pleasure in my grandchildren's achievements, but it would be infinitely greater if I could share the joy with my parents.

So, dad and mom, you may no longer have to do diapers or pay for dental braces. But, oh, how much you are needed! Your roles may have indeed changed, but your value never changes, except, that is, that it increases.

63.

APOLOGIZE? NOT ALWAYS

If you have offended someone, you should make amends and apologize. It is appropriate that you express your regret for having acted thoughtlessly. While such apologies are commendable , there are some that are not.

In a psychotherapy session, the client cried as she related a painful incident. Then, drying her tears with a tissue she said, "I'm sorry for crying."

"Sorry for crying?" I said. "There is no reason to apologize for crying when you are hurting."

"I apologize for everything," she said. "I'm always apologizing."

I pointed out to her that constantly apologizing is indicative of exaggerated and unwarranted guilt feelings that often accompany low self-esteem.. It is almost as though one is trying to justify one's existence. We discussed this at some length, and she said she would be on the alert and try to avoid unnecessary apologies. When her scheduled session was over, she left.

As the client left the room, she saw a man sitting in the waiting room. He was a bit early for his appointment. She promptly blurted out, "I'm sorry for taking so much of the doctor's time."

Some behavior patterns are difficult to change. If you find yourself in the habit of constantly apologizing, think about why you are doing this. You may be suffering from unwarranted feelings of inferiority.

While on the subject of apology, I have been asked whether it is appropriate for parents to apologize to their children when they realize they have done something wrong. Wouldn't this undermine parental authority?

Think for a moment. We want our children to apologize when they have done something wrong. How can they learn this if parents do not teach them this by modeling for them? Don't worry about undermining your authority as parents. It is important that children realize that parents are really human beings after all and as such they are fallible. They often have an image of parents as omniscient, omnipotent, and infallible. This is not true, and such misconceptions may adversely affect parent-child relationships.

Apologize when it is called for, even to children. Do not apologize when it is not called for, even to adults.

64.

CHILDREN: GOING AWAY OR GOING ASTRAY

Children sometimes stray from their parents' lifestyle, and they may even do things that are anathema to them. What should parents do? Should they act in a way that amounts to a rejection of the child because of his/her errant behavior? This may result in a total disruption of their relationship. On the other hand, if they do not object to the behavior, is this not tantamount to approving it? If the parents do not show strong signs of disapproval, is it not possible that siblings may follow suit?

Parents' love for their children is and should be unconditional. Parents should not deceive themselves into believing that they have control over their children. They may influence, but not control.

Parents should take a strong stand when they see their children's behavior as being self-destructive. If, for example, a child is using drugs, the parents must strongly object to it. Many youngsters are not frightened away from use of drugs by the risk of severe damage to their health and future, and they have a thousand ways of justifying their use. The attitude of parents should be, "We love you dearly, and precisely because we love you, we cannot condone your doing things that we know are harmful to you. When you were an infant, we took you to the doctor for immunization. You must have thought that we were being very cruel to you when we had the doctor stab you with a sharp needle. At that time you had no way of knowing that this would protect you from crippling diseases. Your situation now is no different. We will do what we understand is in your best interest, even though you may not agree with us."

Whether it is drugs or any other self-destructive behavior, it is important that parents get expert advice on how to relate to their child. *Expert advice; not from well-meaning relatives and friends, but from people who are credentialed in the management of young people's problems.*

Comments such as "You'll be the death of me," or "If you aggravate your father he may have a heart attack," or "What will people say about us?" or "You are bringing shame on the family" — these are all counterproductive. Such remarks indicate that the parents are not primarily concerned about what the youngster is doing to himself, but rather how he is affecting others. The primary concern should be for the youngster's welfare.

Parents should not take their child's behavior as an indication that he/she does not like them. There are powerful factors, especially peer pressure, that may affect a child's behavior in spite of his love for his parents. Also parents should not jump to the conclusion that they were at fault in raising the child. Children may develop problems in spite of parents' best efforts.

Reaction to children who have behavior problems should not be of the knee-jerk type, but must be well thought out and with proper counseling.

65.

WHO BROKE THE GLASS?

My grandfather noticed a glass standing very near the edge of the table. "Who broke that glass?" he asked. We looked at him with bewilderment. "The glass is not broken," I said. "It is as good as broken," he said. "A very slight jarring of the table will cause it to fall and break. The person who jars the table will not be the one to blame, but rather the person who set the glass in such a precarious place."

What is true of a precarious place for a glass is equally true of our behavior. Sometimes we blame others for our injuries, but if we were to look closer, we may see that we contributed to the injury by unnecessarily placing ourselves at risk.

This holds true for many situations. If we would think prior to speaking, we might find that what we are about to say will very likely elicit a nasty response. Sure, the other person is responsible for what he says and does, but whey should we provoke him?

Some things are predictable. If you put candy within easy reach of children, and they eat it before supper, you are really the one to blame. You should have known that a child cannot resist the temptation for candy.

This is true of adults as well as children. If we provoke someone to improper behavior, we are at least partially at fault. If we place ourselves in a position where we are vulnerable to act improperly, let us then not take shelter behind "He made me do it," or the spurious defense that we were driven by an "irresistible impulse."

Once we are in a vulnerable position and are tempted or provoked, control of our actions may require a great deal of effort. Avoiding situations that are conducive to improper behavior is much easier.

Remember: The glass at the edge of the table, for all practical purposes, is already broken.

66.

BEWARE OF GEOGRAPHIC CURES

There are times when making a geographic change is advisable. A person with a particular marketable skill may be living in a city where there are few jobs available for him, and he could do much better in a different city. A businessman may not be doing well in one location, and his fortune might be much better elsewhere. It is of such situations that the Talmud says that a person should not complain that he is not doing well if he does not take reasonable steps to improve his situation (*Bava Metzia* 75b). There is an aphorism that has an origin in the Talmud: "Change your location and your luck may change" (*Rosh Hashanah* 16b).

This is indeed true, but the same does not apply when a person is dissatisfied with himself or is emotionally distraught. Instead of trying to understand what may be causing him to feel this way and correcting it, he may relocate in the hope that he will feel better elsewhere. We refer to this as a "geographic cure." Very often this does not work, and his condition remains the same. Sometimes, the attempt at a geographic cure may backfire and the person may be worse off than before.

I recall the case of a person who was discontented in his late adolescence, but always found something to which he could attribute his discontent. At first he thought he was in the wrong field in school, so he changed courses. When this did not relieve him, he left school and took a job in sales. His discontent persisted, and he concluded that the companionship of marriage would solve his problem. (It has been aptly said, "Marriage is not a hospital.") As his family grew, there were the myriad of problems common to family life: child illnesses, difficult behavior problems in children, financial pressures, getting the children through college, worrying about their relationships, surviving their weddings (especially the seating arrangements!), helping them get established, etc.. He could always explain why he felt distressed.

At age 55, he was comfortable financially, and his children were married and settled. He still was discontented, and concluded that the house he was living in was to blame. He bought a spacious home in the suburbs. Remodeling and furnishing it provided him with more excuses for his misery. At last everything was finished, and now he would finally be happy!

Of course, since he had never dealt with the real reasons for his discontent, which had been there for forty years, he was as miserable as ever. What was much worse was that he could not find anything to blame anymore. Anything, that is, except his wife. Just as he married in the attempt to shake off the blues, he now divorced for the same reason. Understandably, after the divorce he was more distressed than ever before.

It is so easy to blame one's discontent on external factors and try to manipulate them. This is what may happen with a geographic cure. The underlying causes are not addressed, and the discontent is not resolved.

Except for reasonable moves because of economic considerations, don't fall into the trap of a geographic cure. Get counseling or therapy to try and get to the root of the discontent. Avoid the manipulations. The earlier you deal effectively with the real issues, the easier it will be to resolve them.

67.

LUNCHTIME IS NOT WORKTIME

As I pointed out earlier, I am a stickler for not wasting time, not even a single moment. I don't consider judicious relaxation a waste of time. It is what both the body and mind need for optimal functioning. Anyone who does something just to kill "time" is either terribly foolish or very ignorant. Time is virtually the only commodity that can never be replaced. Why would any sane and sensible person wish to destroy something so valuable?

I used to brown bag lunch. (I had to. There were no kosher facilities in the hospital.) Why waste the precious time of lunch? I always had a pile of medical charts to review, and I would do so while eating my sandwich and drinking coffee.

One day I was studying the Talmud. Jewish law requires that unless an employee has specific permission from his employer he must devote his entire worktime to the task for which he was hired. If he is at work when it is time for the required daily prayers, he is not allowed to recite the full service. He may say only an abbreviated prayer. Prayer is very important in Judaism, but it does not take priority over one's commitment to his employer.

Nevertheless, a worker may interrupt his work and take the necessary time to eat his lunch. He may do so even if the type of work he is doing could be done while eating, just like my reviewing medical records during lunch. Why not require the worker to do so? It would not interfere with his eating.

The answer can only be that the Talmud considers any kind of work to be an interference with eating, even when it is technically possible to do both at the same time. Eating should be relaxing, and work is not relaxing.

I stopped doing chart work during lunch. Instead, I would read something conducive to relaxation. No, lunchtime is not for reading the latest in medical advances nor the stock market report. That's work.

I later came across an article describing the "type A" personality. This describes a person who is always under pressure of time. The "type A" personality is at greater risk of high blood pressure and heart attacks. One example of the "type A" personality, the article said, is someone who works during lunchtime! He is so driven to achieve that he cannot relax when necessary.

There are other ways in which the "type A" personality drives himself. For example, he is likely to do two or even three things at the same time. He is terribly impatient. He may drive aggressively, risking injuring himself and others to get to his destination two minutes faster. If you are a "type A" person, you will do yourself a great favor to change. Do one thing at a time. Don't try and make a left turn quickly and beat the oncoming cars when the light turns green.

Especially, don't work while you're eating lunch.

68.

A KING REMAINS A KING

There is a maxim that states when the chess game is over, the king and the pawn go back into the same box. The message is that the status of the two is different only when they are actively exercising their functions. Otherwise, the great and the small are equal.

A bit of analysis will reveal that this is not quite correct. Even in the box, the king is a king and the pawn is a pawn.

Sometimes things happen in life that cause us to lose our status. A company executive suffers a stroke, and instead of directing a multimillion-dollar corporation, he may be relegated to a sharply restricted lifestyle, perhaps even to a wheelchair. A high government official is displaced from his office. Instead of being a power broker, he is an ordinary citizen. A variety of incidents can topple a person from his pedestal.

Rabbi Chaim Shmulevitz cites a Midrash, that when King Solomon was displaced from his throne by a demon, he wandered from village to village, often begging for food. "Whereas he had previously been king over an enormous realm, he was now king only over his walking staff." Rabbi Shmulevitz comments that although the walking staff was Solomon's only possession, he remained king over it; i.e., Solomon never lost his pride and regal attitude.

A person who had always provided for his family finds himself out of work because his firm downsized. This can be a devastating blow to a person's ego. As distasteful as it is, it should not be allowed to destroy a person's self-esteem. We should not allow circumstances beyond our control to affect our self-concept.

A person must maintain self-esteem even in defiance of social standards. A wealthy man whose advice was frequently sought on community issues suffered a severe reversal and became impoverished. He found that no one consulted him any longer. "It is true that I lost my money," he said, "but I did not lose my wisdom!"

When Solomon roamed the countryside, declaring, "I am Solomon!" people mocked at him and thought him to be insane. Solomon did not allow people's opinion of him to crush him. He knew he was king and he remained king even after he was "put back into the box." He later returned to his throne and became a functional king once again.

Many people experience ups and downs in life. If you allow the "downs" to destroy your self-esteem, you may not be in a position to take advantage of the upswing when it occurs. Even if life's vicissitudes take things from you, they should never be permitted to take "you" away from yourself.

69.

SELF-SACRIFICE IS NOT NECESSARILY NOBLE

Being considerate of others is commendable. Selfishness is loathsome. But taking care of yourself, even sometimes putting yourself first, need not be selfish.

We often hear the statement, "Look out for Number One." This may be interpreted as encouraging self-centeredness, and that would be wrong. However, in the Talmud we find a statement, "your life comes first" (*Bava Metzia* 62a), and the Talmud vigorously discourages selfishness. How are we to understand this?

The great sage Hillel put things in proper perspective in his famous aphorism: "If I am not for myself, who will be for me? And if I am only for myself, of what good am I?" (*Ethics of the Fathers* 1:14).

When you travel on an airplane, you are advised that if there should be a sudden change in cabin pressure, oxygen masks will drop down before you. The airline attendant demonstrates how to put on the mask, and then says: "If you are traveling with a small child, *put your own mask on first, then attend to the child.*" How can one expect a devoted mother to put herself before her child?

The answer is that if the mother tries to put on the child's mask while she may be gasping for air, she is likely not to put the mask on the child properly. Both she and the child will then be without oxygen. If she puts her own mask on first, she will be able to attend properly to the child, and both will be taken care of. In this case, caring for the child first is not noble self-sacrifice, but may actually be a serious mistake.

What the wise Hillel said is that in order to provide for others, you have to be around to do it. If neglecting yourself will result in the inability to do for others, you should take care of yourself first. "If I am not for myself, then who will be for me?" If you don't put on your own oxygen mask first, no one will do it for you and you may become disabled. "If I am only for myself, what good am I? " Once you have put your oxygen mask on, you should look around to see if anyone around you needs help.

I have seen people so very devoted to their spouses and children that they may sometimes neglect themselves in favor of the others. This may indeed be commendable, but it requires careful evaluation. If self-sacrifice can result in harm to oneself, then everyone suffers and no one gains anything.

We may be unable to properly evaluate where caring for oneself ends and selfishness begins. Other people whose judgment is not affected by our emotions may be more objective and put things in proper perspective for us. Asking a competent person for advice can help us avoid misguided self-sacrifice.

70.

A LAUGH A DAY KEEPS MISERY AWAY

We are always on the lookout for ways to feel better. Some medications can relieve a bad mood, while others may prevent it. Here is something that does both, at no cost and without any harmful side effects.

Arrange with a friend to exchange a funny story every day. You may get jokes from books or draw upon your own repertoire. You should agree to be honest and say you've already heard it, and there should always be a back-up joke for such occasions. It's a phone call of only a few minutes at the most, and it can set your mood for the day.

You might even make this arrangement with two or more people. In this way, you can convey the joke you heard from "A" to "B." The few minutes you spend on the phone are by no means a waste of time. A good mood can increase your efficiency and save you hours of work. It is self-explanatory that the jokes should not involve ridicule or mockery but simply be humorous.

In addition to a regularly scheduled humorous conversation, you might also agree that at any time you feel down, you may call each other for a dose of humor. This will require you to be prepared with some additional jokes every day. That's just fine. You'll laugh when you read them and laugh even more when you tell them.

71.

CUT YOUR LOSSES

Sometimes the stuff is so big and heavy that we sweat profusely.

Distraught parents consulted me. Several years after her marriage, their daughter began distancing herself from them. They tried their utmost to restore the relationship, but to no avail. She does not allow them to visit their grandchildren, and has returned the birthday gifts they sent them. A minister who tried to intervene was rebuffed. The parents believe that her husband has turned her against them. They do not know whether he is abusive to her. They have no way of reaching her.

The parents do not wish to pursue the legal path of "grandparents' rights." They think that the grandchildren have been turned against them. What kind of grandparents don't send their grandchildren birthday gifts?

My heart bled for these parents who cried over the loss of their daughter and grandchildren. They had become severely depressed. The father has not been able to practice his profession properly. The mother stopped her community work, and weeps many times during the day. Both parents took antidepressant medication which did not help. No pill could relieve the pain of their loss. They pleaded, "Isn't there anything we can do?"

I responded, "Yes, there is something you can do. You can keep yourself healthy so that you can enjoy your other children and grandchildren and be available to them. Letting yourself deteriorate will not help restore the relationship with your alienated daughter. It will only make things worse for you and your other children."

It is very difficult to accept powerlessness. However, this is sometimes a fact of life. If you hear a cry for help from a person who is drowning, you should do everything possible to save him. If you do not know how to swim, cannot throw him a line, or summon any help, it is senseless to jump into the water and drown with him. That will not do him any good.

Losses are difficult to accept. If you can salvage something, by all means do so. If there is nothing you can do, cut your losses. At least you can save yourself.

72.

FORGIVENESS IS WITHIN REACH

Sometimes we say or do something to someone which we regret. We must apologize and ask for forgiveness. If we caused any damage, we must make restitution. Regret alone is not enough. Repentence is incomplete until we make amends to the person we offended. If that person refuses to accept our amends, he is doing wrong. God will forgive us if we have done everything we can to set things right.

Sometimes we are unable to make amends. What then? Should we carry the guilt forever?

My home phone number is unlisted, but it is the world's worst-kept secret. I frequently receive long distance calls for what amounts to free psychiatric advice. This does not bother me. I am a bit perturbed when the long-distance calls are "collect." I accept these calls because I think that the caller may be on the way to doing something desperate, and may be calling me as a last resort. I don't want to be haunted by the thought that I may have been derelict by not forestalling a disaster.

One evening I came home late from work, and began eating

a late dinner. The phone rang, and the operator said, "I have a call for Dr. Twerski." "Who from?" I asked. I did not recognize the name, but took the call anyway.

The woman's problem was not of an emergency nature. I answered her question, then said very angrily, " This call could have waited until tomorrow. You did not have to bother me at home. But you have some *chutzpah*, reversing the charges!" I then slammed down the receiver.

It later occurred to me that the operator had not asked whether I would accept the charges. The woman had called "person-to-person" but not "collect." I was sorry that I had rebuked her for something she had not done. I wished to apologize for my rudeness, but I did not know who she was and could not reach her. My guilt feelings could not be removed by an apology.

The next two days I was tormented by guilt feelings. I resolved that I would be more careful next time and not be so hasty in rebuking someone. That in itself was not enough. I had no way of getting this woman's forgiveness.

Several days later I read in a book on ethics that if you have offended someone but are not able to reach him to make amends, your sincere regret and intention to apologize are adequate. *God will then put it in that person's heart to forgive you.*

I was relieved. There is no point in harboring guilt feelings when you can't do anything to remedy a wrong. Of course, you must do everything possible to set things right and resolve not to act that way again. You may then be secure in being forgiven.

73.

STRESS CAN BE BENEFICIAL

We hear so much about the need for stress management that we may conclude that all stress is invariably bad. This is not true. If it were not for the stress of needing to support ourselves, many people would stay in bed all day. If it were not for the stress of getting good grades in order to get into a profession, many people would wile away their time instead of studying.

The stress we need to avoid is the kind that hinders our performance. We can build up anxiety to the point where we cannot function properly. This is known as the "William Tell Syndrome."

William Tell was an excellent archer, and was challenged by the king to shoot an arrow at an apple which was placed on his son's head. If his aim failed he might kill his own son. This anxiety could be paralyzing.

If you were told to try and hit the bull's-eye of a target, your hand would be steady on the bow and arrow, and with some luck, you might come close to the bull's-eye. If you were told to shoot at an apple on your son's head, the consequences of failure are so great that it would cause your hands to shake. Any chance of hitting the target would be eliminated by the anxiety.

One bright student had so severe an anxiety about exams that his mind went blank when he took tests. He was the first in a large family to make it to college. He had been made to feel that the family honor depended on his scholastic excellence. The normal stress of an exam gets the adrenaline flowing. The disproportionate importance of the exam was petrifying.

Size things up correctly. Don't exaggerate the importance of things to the point where they become matters of life and death. Blowing things up out of proportion invites failure.

Get some objective evaluation of the challenges confronting you. Your own evaluation of them may be more related to emotional issues than to reality. Keep things in their proper proportion and you'll be able to succeed in your performance.

74.

AN UNLIMITED SUPPLY

We are the recipients of God's benevolence every day. We may not recognize it.

A recovering alcoholic with many years of sobriety was trying to help a newcomer stop drinking. "I can't understand how you have been able to avoid taking a drink for so many years," the novice said. "I find it impossible to stay sober even one week."

The veteran replied, "It's very simple. Every night I thank God for having given me another day of sobriety. I pray that He will give me another day of sobriety tomorrow. That's all there is to it."

"How do you know it was God that gave you that day of sobriety?" the newcomer asked.

The veteran looked at him with puzzlement. "It had to be," he said. "I didn't ask anyone else!"

We tend to take things for granted. We see, hear, speak, use our hands and feet. We act as though these abilities came from nowhere. We may be anxious that the supply will run out.

Knowing that God is the One Who gives us all these things is reassuring. He has an unlimited supply, and will provide for us if we ask for it.

75.

SETBACK OR OPPORTUNITY?

I have often heard the expression, "Whenever you fall down, try to pick something up."

In my study of psychology I read about the concept of "regression in the service of the ego." In plain English this means that we sometimes have to take a step back in order to advance. This was nothing new. Hundreds of years ago, Jewish ethicists wrote about "descending in order to ascend."

When we stand upright, our vision is focused at eye level. Valuable things may be lying in the mud where no one can appreciate their beauty. Furthermore, they may be damaged when people inadvertently step on them. If you have fallen and look around at ground level, you may see things to which you would otherwise have been oblivious.

My work brings me in contact with some people who have "fallen into the mud." Avi is such a person. His drug use led him to stealing and he spent years in jail. I recognized that Avi had potential. There was something intrinsically good about him. We worked with him to peel off the layers that besmirched his soul. I told Avi that he was like an uncut diamond whose beauty was there, but concealed.

Avi stopped using drugs and began a program of recovery in which he learned new values and a different lifestyle. Months later, Avi was hauling some old furniture donated to the treatment center. As he was dragging an old sofa up the stairs, an envelope fell from the cushions. It contained $5000. This was ownerless money, subject to the rule of "finders-keepers." Keeping it would not constitute theft.

Avi called the former owners of the dilapidated furniture and told them about the money. They thanked him and told him to give the money to the treatment center. The former thief had become a philanthropist. Removing the layers that covered his inner soul revealed its beauty.

Avi had a bronze plaque affixed to the door of the treatment center. It says "Diamond Polishing Center."

Sometimes we experience adversity: a business failure, illness, disappointment, and a broken relationship. These painful experiences may allow us to better empathize with others in distress. They may shake us up and set us to think more seriously about what mistakes we may have made and what we really want out of life.

I had found Avi in the mud. I don't recommend intentionally getting down into the mud. However, if you happen to fall, be sure to look around. You may discover something valuable that you would not have seen otherwise.

76.

MAKING WISE DECISIONS

One of the mysteries of life is why God arranged it so that we get our maximum wisdom when we need it least. We accumulate wisdom not only through study, but even more through the experiences we encounter in life. As we grow older, we learn more and more about what works and what does not work, what has real value and what has only an illusory value. By the time we are 70, we are wise and seasoned.

But alas! We do not make the most important decisions of life when we are 70. By that time we are retired from work and maybe spending much time on a rocking chair. Rather, we make our momentous decisions in our late adolescence or early adulthood. That is when we decide whom we marry, what occupation to choose, where to live, etc. Is it not ironic that we make these important decisions when we are least equipped for them? It would seem preferable that we have our maximum wisdom when we are young, energetic, and carefree. If we are impetuous we are more likely to make unwise decisions than when we reach old age.

It must be that the makeup of the human being is such that maximum energy and maximum wisdom cannot both exist at the same time. The only reasonable thing is therefore for young people to allow their tremendous energy to be guided by the wisdom of those who are older and more experienced. This would be ideal, but unfortunately it is no longer popular to take advice from one's elders. Ever since the 1960s, it is not the "in" thing. Young people often expend their tremendous energy according to the limited wisdom of youth. When they are older, they may realize some of the mistakes they made, but by then the past is unretrievable. Life may indeed be tough. Young people could make it less tough by avoiding some of the pitfalls of life. The older folks who have already traveled that road are likely to know where those pitfalls are. Young people would do well to listen to them.

77.

ENJOY YOUR FOOD

Ben and Joe came from the same town in Europe. Ben was a shrewd businessman, and had developed a flourishing laundry business. In the days prior to Laundromats, wash and wear clothes, and disposables, this was a very profitable business. Joe operated a small corner grocery and barely made ends meet.

Ben suffered from stomach ulcers. Prior to modern advances in treatment, the ulcer patient had to subsist on the blandest of bland diets. He often could eat little more than crackers and milk.

One time the two met at an event. Ben embraced Joe and asked, "How are things with you, Joe?"

Joe heaved a sigh. "What can I tell you, Ben? It's not good. I have to get up before dawn to be at the wholesale market early. I have to lift heavy boxes and I stand on my feet all day waiting on customers. After all is said and done, I earn just enough to afford dark bread and black radish for dinner. This is no life, Ben."

"You are a fool, Joe," Ben said. "If only I could eat dark bread and black radish, I would gladly give away half of my business for that privilege."

You may be frustrated by the bills that pile up. You may worry about how you are ever going to get out of debt. Before you get carried away with such worries, think a moment about what you ate yesterday and what you may eat today. There are people who may have many millions of dollars who would feel blessed if only they could eat what you eat.

Don't be foolish. Enjoy your food, and consider yourself blessed.

78.

CRITICISM: CONSTRUCTIVE OR DESTRUCTIVE?

Praise is pleasant. Criticism is unpleasant. Ice cream tastes good. Some medicines taste terrible. We must sometimes accept the unpleasant taste of medicine for its curative powers, and we should accept constructive criticism even if it is unpleasant.

We should avoid making disparaging remarks, but we should not refrain from offering well-intended criticism. We probably learn best from our mistakes, but at times we have to be made aware that we have indeed been mistaken.

The very same words may be said with a benevolent intent or a malevolent intent. How can we distinguish constructive criticism from destructive criticism? This is an important distinction for both givers and receivers of criticism.

Here is a rule of thumb: If the person who makes the criticism is willing to assist the other person in correcting the defect or problem, the criticism is constructive. If not, then his intent is not benign. As parents we often point out to our children that they are doing wrong, but we are interested in helping them do things right. The same attitude accompanies all constructive criticism.

Before you point out a person's shortcoming, ask yourself, "Am I willing to help this person correct or overcome the problem?" If you are not willing to offer help or at least direct the person to a source of help, you should leave the criticism to someone who is willing. Similarly, if the person who criticizes you says his piece and walks off, you may assume that his intent was not constructive. Even in this case, you would be wise to think about the comment. Even though his intent was not benevolent, his observation may have been valid.

79.

LACK OF SUCCESS IS NOT EQUIVALENT TO FAILURE

"**Y**ou have such great potential!" How many times have you heard that? Or perhaps your report card read, "Naomi has great potential. Her grades are far beneath her potential."

Why do some people fail to actualize their potential? One person said, "Ever since I was a child I heard that I had great potential. I was an underachiever. I never got good grades, and this was especially painful because my brother's grades were always good. I felt terrible about myself. My only consolation was that I had good potential, and I held on to that for dear life. I couldn't risk really trying to achieve anything, because if I failed, that would mean that I didn't even have potential. My only redeeming feature would be gone."

Some people may not believe that they have potential. Some may have been told the equivalent of "you'll never amount to anything," and all the reassurances about having potential are futile. Others, like the above person, may believe that they do have potential, but the risk that a failure will disprove this makes it too hazardous to try and develop it.

Telling a child that he has potential should be accompanied by an explanation. Remember the phrase, "Thar's gold in them thar hills"? People who believed there was gold in the hills set out to get rich. They sometimes dug in the ground or panned the river for days and weeks before they struck gold.

Having potential does not mean that one will immediately succeed. There can be a number of failures before one "strikes gold." *Lack of success is not equivalent to failure.* It simply means that one has to keep on trying.

Children should be rewarded for their effort, not for the results. Then they will not fear developing their potential.

80.

BRIEF IS BETTER

We have mentioned several aspects of good communication. There is yet another: brevity. Long-windedness sharply reduces attentiveness.

This is especially true in public speaking. It is much better for the audience to complain about the brevity of a speech: "I could have listened to him for hours" is much better than, "I wish he would not have talked so long."

One lecturer spoke for 1½ hours. When he finished, a member of the audience said to him, "I was very impressed by your speech. I am a television producer and I would like to bring your message to millions of people. However, you know that each second of television time is very costly. Do you think you could condense the essence of your speech into three minutes?"

The speaker thought for a moment, then said, "Yes, I think I could."

"Then why in heaven's name didn't you do so?" he demanded.

Another speaker was once asked how long it would take him

to prepare a five minute talk. "About two or three days," he said. "And how long for a half-hour talk?" "About eight hours," he responded. "And how much preparation would you need for a 1½-hour talk?" "I'm ready right now," he said.

We should have a clear idea just what point it is that we wish to make. We should then write down our speech. Then we should review it and trim away unessential words and sentences. We will not only be brief, but also much more convincing. This is equally true of ordinary conversation. The clearer we are about what we wish to say, the briefer and more impressive we can be.

81.

DO YOU LOOK HOW YOU FEEL OR FEEL HOW YOU LOOK?

It is only normal to wish to be good looking and attractive. One of the major industries is based on people's desire to look nice. Just think of the billions of dollars spent on cosmetics, weight loss, hair styling, wigs, toupees, plastic surgery, and stylish clothes.

Okay. External appearance is important. But it is not everything. Some people who are handsome may feel that they are nothing but decorative, and may neglect developing their intellect and skills, relying totally on their external appearance.

On the other hand, some people may have an unjustified feeling that they are unattractive or even homely. This may be the result of their feeling that they are unworthy or sinful; i.e., "ugly" inside. They then project these feelings outwardly and come to believe that they *look* ugly. I have met people who are stunningly handsome who have a delusion that they are unattractive.

One young woman was convinced that she was ugly and that

191

only surgery to reconstruct her nose could make her more attractive. She consulted several plastic surgeons who refused to do the operation because there was nothing that needed correction. She ultimately found an unscrupulous surgeon, who simply for the fee, was willing to operate on her.

After she recovered from the plastic surgery she became preoccupied with the color of her eyes. If only she could have contact lenses that would change the color of her eyes she would not be ugly. As one might expect, she did not feel any less ugly when she acquired a variety of colored contact lenses.

We must be cautious not to transform the way we feel about ourselves into an opinion of whether we are attractive or unattractive to others. If someone tells you that you are good looking, believe it. If you don't think so, you might benefit from a more correct self-awareness. You may have a pleasant discovery that you are pretty both outside and inside.

82.

OVERWHELMING? THAT DEPENDS

How important something is to someone is obviously relative. A poor man who loses a dollar may be devastated. A rich man who loses a dollar may not give it a second thought.

When we see people react, we must always bear in mind that they may be reacting to what something means to *them*, rather than what it may mean to us. An infant may cry because someone took away his yellow ball. A grownup may be very upset because his Cadillac was stolen. The infant's response is as reasonable as the grownup's.

In a state mental hospital, one woman beat another because the latter had put a toothbrush into her cubicle. The nurse thought her reaction was uncalled for. I pointed out that this woman had nothing in the world that she could claim as her own private space. She slept in a ward with 40 beds. She ate meals in a cafeteria with hundreds of women like her. She wore the dresses that the hospital dispensed, all of which looked alike. The only space in the world that was exclusively her own was the tiny cubicle where she kept her personal things. The other woman's placing her toothbrush there was equivalent to breaking into someone's home.

If the wind blows a cinder into your eye, you will feel *very* uncomfortable. When it is removed on the cotton of a Q-Tip it appears almost microscopic in size. When it was lodged in your eye it felt like a mountain. Why? Because it irritated a highly sensitive area.

We often pass judgment on others without knowing all the facts. The Talmud says, "Do not judge another person until you have reached his place" (*Ethics of the Fathers* 2:5). Since we can never totally identify with anyone, we should be extremely wary of being judgmental.

83.

BE IN TOUCH WITH YOUR FEELINGS

It may be wrong to generalize. However, some things happen with sufficient frequency that some generalization is justifiable.

I have often seen people react with emotions that seem improper. I have seen men become enraged when anger was not in place, and I have seen women cry when an angry response would have been appropriate.

Some men have the idea that it is not macho for men to cry. Men should be made of sterner stuff. They should be strong and not let things or people hurt them. When someone does hurt them they convert the pain to anger and may act out in rage. Some women, on the other hand, may think that it is not feminine to show anger. Instead of allowing themselves to feel angry, they cry.

I'm *not* recommending acting out in rage, but you should be able to identify your feelings. We are capable of controlling our expression of anger, but we can only do so if we are aware of what we are feeling. Feeling hurt instead of angry may result in feeling sorry for yourself instead of acting constructively. Similarly, acting out in rage when you are really hurting badly can be very destructive.

It is a mistake to think how we should *feel* when we are hurt or provoked. We are responsible for our *actions* and *behavior*. We are not responsible for our *feelings*. If we correctly identify our feelings, we can react appropriately.

Sometimes we say, "You shouldn't feel that way." This is correct when we feel hurt or provoked because we misperceived or misunderstood something. For example, we did not hear correctly, and we may think someone made an unkind remark. Or, a person may have said something he didn't really mean. Our feelings may have been justified if we had indeed been wronged. It is not uncommon to misperceive or misunderstand, and we should give people the benefit of the doubt.

When your feelings are justified, don't deny them. Acknowledging them will give you much better control of your reactions.

84.

ALONE OR LONELY?

Some people enjoy a period of solitude. It allows them to think without being distracted or interrupted by goings on in their environment. Loneliness, on the other hand, is a feeling that no one ever enjoys.

One prominent psychiatrist noted that although much has been written about a variety of human emotions, there is relatively little in the psychologic literature about loneliness. He hypothesized that loneliness is a frightening feeling, and may cause so much anxiety in psychiatrists and psychologists that they avoid the subject.

What is the difference between being alone or being lonely? Being alone means that you do not have *anyone else* near you. Being lonely means that you do not have your *self*. In other words, loneliness is an alienation from oneself, and this is indeed a most distressing feeling.

You may be totally alone, out in the woods with no one around for miles, yet you may be at peace with yourself. The absence of distraction actually allows you to focus more on yourself and to come closer with yourself. This enhances your self-awareness, and you welcome it. While you are indeed alone, you are not lonely.

On the other hand, you may be in a sports stadium among 50,000 people, yet you may be terribly lonely. The action on the playing field may temporarily distract you from your misery, but in the moments that you are not distracted, you may feel very uncomfortable.

If we live our lives in a way that we can feel good about ourselves, as when we do things for others and develop commendable character traits, we need never become alienated from ourselves. We can enjoy knowing who we are, and when we are totally alone, we are in pleasant company: ourselves. We need never again suffer the pangs of loneliness.

85.

DON'T BE AFRAID TO ACCEPT HELP

Many people will readily help others. It is indeed a good feeling and a meritorious act to help someone. Accepting help, on the other hand, is another story.

A woman who was eight months into recovery from alcoholism related that her furnace had broken down during a frigid spell. It was not repaired for several days, and she slept in an unheated apartment. Some friends told her that she could have spent the few days with them. "Oh, no," she said. "I don't like to impose myself on anyone."

I asked the woman to come to my office. "You were doing so well in recovery that I had hoped to call on you for help with newcomers," I said.

"You can call on me anytime, Doctor," she said. "I'll be more than happy to help anyone."

"I'm sorry," I said. "If you cannot accept help, then you have no right to give it."

Some people think that giving help is a sign of a mature personality. Perhaps. However, a person whose self-esteem is not threatened by *accepting* help may be at a higher level of maturity. The Talmud is very critical of someone who refuses legitimate help.

Of course, one should not be a parasite and expect the world to take care of his needs. But if one really is in need of help, one should not be a martyr and refuse it.

86.

KEEP YOUR EYE ON THE WHITE LINE

Several years ago I drove to the Catskills, and I ran into a dense fog just as it was beginning to get dark. But this was just not any fog. By comparison, London fogs are clear as crystal. The only way I can describe it is that it reminded me of the plague of darkness in Egypt, which is described as being so thick that the darkness was palpable.

I don't recall ever feeling so terrified before or after. I could not see the taillights of the car in front of me, and by the same token, the driver behind me could not see my taillights. I could not drive ahead for fear of hitting the car ahead of me, nor could I stop because I would be hit by the car in back of me. I could not pull over and wait for the fog to disperse because I had no idea what was at the side of the road, and I might end up in a ditch. Looking through the windshield was as futile as trying to look through a brick wall.

However, looking through the side window I could make out a white line at the edge of the road. I kept my eye on the white line and inched along, keeping myself parallel to the white line. Eventually I emerged from the fog and was able to reach my destination.

Not infrequently we may find ourselves in a dense fog, not one that is outside of us, but one that is within our minds. Circumstances in life may throw us into a state of confusion, and we may be in a dilemma about what to do. We may be afraid to proceed, we may be afraid to back up, we may be afraid to stand still, and we may be afraid to make a turn. This can be extremely anxiety provoking.

However, there is a "white line" that can serve as a guide to safety. If we cannot see things clearly when we look for ourselves, we must turn to the Eternal guide. For Jews this is the Torah which includes not only Scripture, the Talmud, and the laws, but also all the writings on ethical behavior. If we do not have access to them on our own or cannot find the answer to our problem, consultation with a Torah authority can help us resolve it.

Keeping our eye on the "white line" of Torah and letting it be our guide can get us out of the "fog" safely.

87.

HAVE MERCY ON FOOLS

Unfortunately there are people who are fools, and they may be very annoying company. It takes a great deal of restraint to keep from telling them to please be quiet and not expose their stupidity to everyone. Yet, keep quiet you must, because to say anything of the sort would be humiliating. It is a grave sin to humiliate someone.

So there you are, compelled to keep quiet while this person keeps saying things that can make your blood boil. You may become very angry at this person for 1) saying such stupid things, and 2) putting you in a position where every last bit of your patience may be exhausted.

It is not good to feel angry. There is a way in which you can lessen your anger.

The Talmud states that before a person's birth, it is actually decreed in heaven whether he will be wise or dull. If someone is dull, do not hold it against him. This is the lot he was dealt. It is not his fault.

However, you may contend that he could have complied with the heavenly decree by being just a little bit foolish. Why does he have to be so great a fool?

Some people are perfectionistic. When they are assigned a task, they give it their utmost. This person simply wished to make sure that he was in full compliance.

So, why be angry at him? It is not his fault that he is a fool in the first place, and the magnitude of his folly is due to his trying to fulfill his assignment to the greatest degree possible. Can you be angry at a person for being a perfectionist?

So have mercy on a fool. If you insist that you must also have mercy on yourself, try some of the antinudnik techniques.

88.

POWER CAN BE SEDUCTIVE

Power can be real or illusory. Both may be seductive and destructive.

People who use cocaine report that it gives them a feeling of incomparable strength. They become supermen. This sense of power comes at an exorbitant cost.

A person may attain real power by achieving a position of dominance. He may control the lives of employees, clients, or patients. He may control an army and have an arsenal of awesome weapons.

Real power can be as seductive as the illusory power of cocaine. Some people are never satisfied with the level of power they have attained, and their lust for power is insatiable. Their pursuit of power may come at the expense of their health, of their families, and of those whom they seek to control.

The Talmudic definition of power is a very healthy one. "The powerful person is one who is master over himself" (*Ethics of the Fathers* 4:1).

Don't seek to control others. Achieving mastery over one's own impulses is enough to keep one occupied an entire lifetime. This kind of mastery is both healthy and conducive to happiness.

89.

LEARNING TO PRAY

Rabbi Shneur Zalman was once asked why he became a disciple of the Maggid of Mezeritch. He was already an accomplished Torah scholar at the time. Rabbi Shneur Zalman said, "I heard that in Mezeritch they teach how to pray. I already knew something about learning, but I knew very little about praying."

The "very little" of Rabbi Shneur Zalman is far greater than our "very much." Some people today, albeit on a different level, also have trouble with praying. "I can't concentrate," they may say. Or, "I don't have any feeling when I pray." Or, "I pray, but it is just a ritual with me."

We often pray for good health, for a livelihood, for pleasure from our children. We pray for these things because they are our *needs*. When we want something, we pray for it. If, God forbid, we are sick, we pray even more intensely for health. The quality of our prayer depends on how much we recognize our needs.

The ability to pray properly is very important. We should recognize that we have a need to pray. Just as we pray for other needs, we should pray for the knowledge of *how to pray*.

In many of the more comprehensive prayer books there is a beautiful composition by Rabbi Elimelech of Lizhensk, "A Prayer Before Praying." He asks God to remove the obstacles that stand in the way of prayer and to help him pray properly. Reciting this prayer can improve the quality of our prayer.

You may say: Isn't a bit strange to pray for the ability to pray? It is not strange at all. Don't we have appetizers before a meal to stimulate our desire to eat? If we have appetizers to help us have a better appetite, why not a prayer to help us pray better?

If we realize that we are not praying as well as we should, that means we recognize that we have a need to pray better. Let us pray, then, for help with that need.

90.

KEEP AN OPEN MIND

We may not realize that sometimes we pay a steep price for being closed minded. You've heard it said, "Don't talk logic to me. My mind is made up." That happens far too often.

Sure, we should have our convictions and we should not be swayed by every fad. But we should listen.

Our minds are capable of analyzing things and coming to a conclusion. We can only give proper consideration to ideas if we let them enter our minds. If we close our minds we may miss valuable advice.

Some people close their minds precisely because they are afraid that if they allow an idea to enter, they may discover it is correct. This may necessitate a change in their behavior. We are creatures of habit. We dislike change. We may therefore reject anything that may lead to change.

The prophet Isaiah stated this clearly: "These people have closed their ears because they fear that if they hear they will have to change their ways."

Don't close your mind. We should always be in search of the truth, and accept it wherever it may lead us. As long as you are in sincere pursuit of truth, listening to other opinions is never harmful.

91

DUST TO DUST – SO WHAT!

The other day at the drugstore I met a friend who appeared very disgruntled, muttering and grumbling under his breath. Upon inquiring the reason for his anger, he told me that he had purchased an instant lottery ticket and won ten dollars. He kept one dollar and bought nine more tickets and won nothing. "Can you imagine that?" he said. "Nine tickets and not even a free ticket winner'".

"You shouldn't be complaining," I said. "You invested a dollar, got your dollar back, and had the fun of scratching off nine more tickets. You came out ahead."

Don't get me wrong. I'm not advocating gambling. I'm merely pointing out that we may sometimes get upset because we think we have lost something, while we really haven't lost anything.

This reminds me of a man who was tearfully reciting the Yom Kippur prayers. "Why are you crying?" another worshipper asked.

The man pointed to the prayer book. "Just look at what it says here. Man comes from dust and will turn into dust.' That is so sad."

The second worshipper said, "Not at all. You see, if man were made of gold and turned into dust, that would indeed be tragic. But if he begins as dust and ends up as dust, and between the two he can make a *l'chaim,* that's pure profit."

I don't advocate drinking (to excess, that is) any more than gambling. However, the point is well taken. We should look at our starting point. If we look at things from this perspective we may find that many things are not grounds for feeling dejected. To the contrary, they may even be grounds for feeling cheerful.

92.

PUTTING HUMPTY DUMPTY TOGETHER

H umpty Dumpty sat on a wall.
Humpty Dumpty had a great fall.
All the king's horses and all the king's men
Couldn't put Humpty Dumpty together again.

You know what the real problem with Humpty Dumpty was? He relied on the king's horses and the king's men to fix him. If Humpty Dumpty had tried to put himself together, he might have recovered from the damage of a great fall.

A man came to the Rabbi of Shiniv and asked that the Rabbi intercede and pray for him that he should be virtuous and not sin. The Rabbi closed his eyes as if in deep meditation, then said to him, " I have successfully interceded for you and my prayers have been accepted. God is completely agreeable that you should be virtuous and not sin. The rest is up to you."

There are indeed situations where we may require others to set us straight. We may need the skills of craftsmen or professionals to do for us what we cannot do for ourselves. However, there is much that we *can* do to refine our character. While we may need guidance from others, we must do the work ourselves.

I recall that when I was a child I told my tutor, "I have no objection to being learned. If there was a machine that could put all the information into my head, I would be overjoyed. I just don't want to spend time learning when I could be having fun with my friends."

Unfortunately, there is no learning machine, nor is there any character-building machine. No one will do it for us, not even God. Learning and character building are things you must do for yourself.

Do make the effort. The rewards are great.

93.

DON'T EXTRAPOLATE

There is a folk saying, "Someone who burns his tongue on hot soup will blow on cold soup."

Sometimes we act inappropriately because we make incorrect assumptions. A bowl of hot soup may have indeed caused a person pain. He may therefore develop the fear that *all* bowls of soup are too hot.

You may have experienced something unpleasant in one setting. It is possible that you may think of other situations as unpleasant because they bear some similarity to the unpleasant one. Actually they may be very different. The comparison may be unjustified.

A person who suffered a painful rejection in a relationship may be frightened away from *all* relationships. He may sentence himself to a life of loneliness. An early trauma at the hands of an authority figure may cause a person to detest all authority.

Don't allow yourself to be a captive of past experiences. Learn to evaluate each situation on its own merits.

94.

YOU ARE MORE OKAY THAN NOT

I was invited to give several lectures to a class of 110 counselors who were taking a course for their continuing education requirements. In order to get credit, the attendees had to complete a questionnaire, evaluating the course material and the lecturers. One month later I received a packet of 110 evaluation forms.

As I read the evaluations, my ego went through the ceiling. There were many flattering comments on my presentation: 109 evaluations praised my performance! However, there was one evaluation that was sharply critical. I felt crushed, and for two weeks I moped. Someone had disapproved of me!

It wasn't until the third week that it struck me that 109 to 1 is not a bad score. One hundred nine people could not be wrong. The lone dissenter was probably not feeling well that day and was seeing everything in a negative light. His criticism of me was probably due to his own unpleasant disposition.

Some people are very sensitive to criticism. I believe that the way I felt those two weeks is the way many people feel when they are criticized. Their feelings are no more justified than mine were.

It is only natural that when you have a pain in the finger, you focus on just that part of the body that hurts. You do not think that your heart, lungs, liver, eyes, and ears are functioning flawlessly. This is equally true when one has a single painful emotion. One negative feeling may obscure all the positive ones.

That is not the way things should be. If you discover or you are told that you did something wrong, you should not be devastated. To the contrary, you should realize that there is far more that is right about you than there is wrong. If you do have some defect, you can correct this and increase your positivity. If you focus only on the pain or on the wrong, you will have lost a valuable opportunity for growth.

In fact, criticism should actually be uplifting. No one bothers to point out a defect in a piece of junk. You should realize that awareness of a defect is an indication that you are more okay than not.

95.

WISDOM OR PROPHECY: WHICH WOULD YOU CHOOSE?

Some people would argue that prophecy is superior to wisdom. There have been many wise people in the world, but only a few true prophets. Accurately predicting the future is certainly an unusual ability.

The Talmud says otherwise: "A wise person is superior to a prophet" (*Bava Basra* 12a). Why? Think a moment. If a prediction of the future is true, there is nothing that can be done to change it. If it is changeable, then the prediction is not correct. If you correctly foresee the future, that does not make any demands of you. The present, however, is subject to change. You must indeed be wise to size up the present correctly and to know what you must do to improve it.

Some people are preoccupied with the past. Others would like to know what the future holds for them. Neither the past nor the future are under our control. We can do something about the present. We should therefore seek to understand the present and find out what we can do to make it better both for ourselves and others.

96.

SOME FEARS ARE GOOD FOR YOU

Fear has gotten a bad press. Psychologists have pointed out that anxiety is at the root of all emotional symptoms. Because fear and anxiety are so similar, some people think that in order to be psychologically healthy a person should not have any fears.

There is a story about a man who refused to go to sleep in his bed because there was an alligator under it. He was taken to a psychiatrist who treated him for this alligator phobia. After an extended period of treatment, he was cured from this phobia and went to sleep in his bed, and an alligator ate him. Fear is unhealthy only when it is groundless.

A recovering alcoholic with seven years of sobriety complained that he was still bothered by the fear that he might slip and drink. "Good!" I said. "Stay that way."

People with phobias of situations that are not in any way dangerous should indeed seek psychological help. However, we should fear that we may do wrong. We are always subject to temptation and we are vulnerable to do things that can provide us with pleasure, even if they are wrong. Fear of doing wrong helps us keep up our guard. This is what Scripture means, "Fortunate is the person who always fears" (*Proverbs* 28:14). Fear of doing wrong is healthy.

97

WATCH OUT FOR
DISTORTED PERCEPTIONS

O ccasionally I suffer from severe migraine headaches. When a headache me in its clutches, the pain is excruciating and I may experience some discomfort for several days. The pain medications do not relieve all of it.

It is one thing to be in pain. I am also aware that right now I am the center of my own world. I am totally preoccupied with my discomfort, and I have little room for feelings for anyone else. I am of course terribly impatient with my pain, but I also notice that this impatience has spread and that I am impatient with everything else and with everyone else. Things that I would usually take in stride are much more irritating and intolerable.

Luckily, I am aware of this, and I know that right now I should keep quiet and not react to things that provoke me. I should also avoid making decisions when my perception of the world is so skewed that instead of the universe consisting of super galaxies billions of light years across, it consists only of the right side of my head. As ridiculous as it seems, I am likely to approach major issues, even decisions that may affect hundreds of people or involve millions of dollars, with the attitude of "How would that make my head feel better?" This may sound absurd, but let me assure you that our minds do not always operate according to the laws of logic, and we may make unwise decisions because of a distorted perspective.

It is not only physical pain that can distort things for us. Emotional pain and exhaustion may cause even greater distortions. Furthermore, whereas we can readily identify physical pain and realize that we are temporarily out of sorts, we may lack this insight when the distress is emotional. When people are depressed they may have a very morbid perception. I recall one successful businessman who was depressed, and was convinced that his business was going to fail because of the money he owed, and that this would be ruinous to his family. He could not get himself to go to the office because of the impending disaster. I spoke with his partner who said, "There's nothing unusual about our situation. Each year at this time we have a large inventory at which time we owe money, and then we sell it and make a handsome profit. There's no reason to think that this year will be any different." The partner's perception was objective, whereas the patient could see only the negatives and was unable to see the positives.

If you are in a bad mood or are hurting physically, delay making important decisions, or at least run them by someone who can be more objective. You'll have nothing to regret when you feel better.

98

BOOK THE PRESIDENT'S ROOM

We may not be spending enough time with the family. We may not spend enough time on the spiritual pursuits. We are so busy with our business and professional responsibilities that we cannot find a free moment for these things.

A tourist once came to a motel whose sign declared "No Vacancy." He asked for a room and was told that there were none available.

"You have over 300 rooms in this motel," he said. "There must be an available room."

"I'm sorry, sir," the clerk said. "All the rooms are taken."

"Don't tell me that if the President of the United States pulled up tonight you wouldn't find a room for him," the man said.

"Well," the clerk said, "for the President we would have to make an accommodation."

"Good!" the man said. "The President is not coming. You can give me his room."

You don't have enough time for the family because you are so occupied with your work. What would happen if, God forbid, you had a heart attack and could no longer put in all those hours at work? You would make do with less time for work, wouldn't you?

Thank God you have not had a heart attack. Reduce your work hours as if you did. Spend more time with the family. You do have the time. You just don't know it.

Book the President's room.

99.

IS IT FEAR OF SUCCESS OR OF FAILURE?

I'm sure you've heard it said, "He always seems to do things in order to fail. He has a fear of success." I found that hard to understand. Fear of failure makes sense, but why would anyone fear success?

My father used to tell a story. In elementary school in the old country, teachers would hit students who misbehaved or were lazy. One time a man saw a teacher asking a child to name the first letter of the Hebrew alphabet. The child was silent. "Name that letter!" the teacher demanded. No answer. The teacher hit the child and repeated his command. Again silence, followed by another slap. After several futile demands and blows, the teacher gave up.

The onlooker asked the child, "Don't you know the name of that letter?"

"That's an *aleph*," the child said.

"Why didn't you tell that to your teacher and avoid the beatings?" the man asked.

"Because," the child said, "if I told him the *aleph*, he would want to know the *beis*, and then the *gimmel* and all the rest. I just put a stop to it at the beginning." My father explained, "Sometimes a person may accept a punishment in the beginning to avoid going on."

My father was right. There are people who are afraid of responsibility. Success at a venture invariably leads to expansion of one's business or duties, which brings additional responsibilities. Some people may anticipate failure and are so devastated by the thought of failing that they sabotage their venture to get it over with. I know of people who have lost valuable relationships by precipitating a rejection. They did this because it was easier for them to get the rejection over with than living with the suspense of waiting for the inevitable rejection. If you don't say the *aleph* you don't have to go on to the rest of the alphabet.

Fear of success is fear of responsibility and really fear of failure.

It is easy to blame failure on external factors. If you find yourself having a pattern of failure, don't simply find something to blame. Review your actions with a competent counselor or therapist. He may help you discover that you *can* succeed. You may need some help in overcoming the fear and anticipation of failure. Once you get rid of these, success can be sweet.

100.

IT'S A MISTAKE TO COMPOUND A MISTAKE

A woman who was severely depressed consulted me. She had been an alcoholic since her adolescence, and now at age 35, sobered up for the first time. Her husband had left her and seemingly disappeared off the face of the earth. Her mind was now clear enough to realize that her seven-year-old son had a mental handicap because she drank during pregnancy. She said she was unable to live with herself. To think that she had brought this child into the world, and that he would have to go through his entire life with a serious disadvantage and not be able to find happiness, was just too much to bear. As long as she had been drinking, she had never thought about this. Now she is constantly reminded of this, and feels so terribly guilty that she has been thinking of suicide.

"Although your son is at a disadvantage, there is still much that he can do. With the proper help he can maximize his potential and indeed find happiness in life. If you take yourself out of the picture, who will care for him? You can find the best programs to help him advance, but without you, he may be relegated to some community agency or institution where he will never maximize his potential.

"Yes, your drinking during pregnancy was a serious mistake. Are you now going to compound that mistake by depriving your son of his only chance to develop his potential?

"You referred to your dereliction of responsibility in bringing him into the world. You are therefore duty bound to do whatever you can for him. Of course your awareness of his handicap is painful to you, and you would escape that pain by suicide. Abandoning him in order to relieve your pain would be the ultimate of selfishness."

This case should serve as an example for those situations where something we did wrong resulted in a negative consequence. In such situations, we naturally feel guilty for our misdeed. If we wish to do the right thing, we should try to the best of our ability to minimize the harmful effects of our act. To escape or in any way avoid dealing with it is adding one mistake on top of another.

When we realize we have done wrong and that there is not much that we can do to totally or even partially undo the result of our act, we should see what there is that we *can* do, both in repenting and in trying to mitigate the unfortunate result. In the case cited above, the mother could obtain the best resources to develop the child's potential to the fullest. In each case there may be something we can do, and we must investigate what that may be. There is never a time when we should resign ourselves to despair or to doing nothing.

101

YOU'RE NEVER TOO OLD TO LEARN

After working for the same company for twenty-seven years, your job is being phased out. They no longer need draftsmen, and the graphics at which you were expert are now being done by a computer. The company offers to train you for something else. You feel that at age fifty-two you cannot learn anything new. You are too set in your ways to change. Your mind can't absorb anything new.

Wrong. Learning something new may not come as easy as at age twenty, but it is not impossible.

The Talmud states that Rabbi Akiva was illiterate at age forty. His wife encouraged him to get an education, but he felt it was futile. Even if he was able to learn new material, he felt he could not retain it and integrate it.

One day he came across a deep groove in a rock that had been formed by water dripping on it for many years. Rabbi Akiva reasoned, "If water can make an impression on hard rock, then certainly the Torah can make an impression on my brain." He began by learning the alphabet, and eventually progressed to become the greatest sage of his era.

We should never despair of learning. We may think that our brain is "hard as a rock." Let us remember, even a rock can yield to pressure. Something as soft as water can cause an impression on a hard rock if it persists.

We may have to tackle new learning at later years. It may seem difficult, but if we persist at it, we can learn and we can retain. Never give up on your educability.

102.

LET YOUR APPRECIATION BE COMPLETE

We often appreciate favors and kindness. Sometimes our appetites may be insatiable. Instead of appreciating what we have, we may be resentful because of what we don't have.

A mother was walking along the oceanfront with her small child. A sudden storm broke out, and before she could get away from the shore, a huge wave tore the child away from her and carried him out to sea. The woman was totally helpless and panicked. In desperation she called out to God: "Please, God, give me back my child!" The very next moment another huge wave came ashore and deposited her child at her feet, safe and sound.

The woman embraced and kissed her child. She raised her eyes toward heaven. "Oh, thank You, God. Thank You." Then she looked at the child, again lifted her eyes toward heaven and again addressed God. This time her tone of voice was less supplicant. "He was wearing a hat," she said.

We are often the beneficiaries of kindness. Sometimes we are remiss in our appreciation because we feel we have more coming to us. We may even focus on a trivia we lack instead of on the food we received.

Let us not ask for the hat.

EPILOGUE

Sometimes the world may look like a very inhospitable place to be. It is full of challenges and hurdles to overcome. Some may be small, some may be big, and some may be immense.

How shall we conceptualize the world we live in? Is it the best of all possible worlds or the worst of all possible worlds? There is enough good in the world that we cannot think of it as the worst. On the other hand, there is enough of the "big stuff" that makes it difficult to think of it as the best.

One thing is clear. There is much about this world that leaves room for improvement. In other words, it would be the worst of all possible worlds except for the fact that *we can make it better.* True, we cannot do anything about the weather other than to predict it. But since man is the ultimate of creation, the essence of the world is not the sun, moon, and stars, but mankind. We can make *ourselves* better, and we can therefore make the world better.

What makes us think of the world as bad is all the hardships we endure: the big ones and the little ones. One recovering person said, "They told me that if I stopped drinking, things would get better. Well, I stopped drinking and things did *not* get better. *I* got better." By coping with life's challenges instead of avoiding them, we minimize these hardships. By reducing the negatives we increase the positives.

Once we begin to move toward the positive we can pick up momentum. The strength we gather from doing this can allow us to advance to dazzling heights.

In the past few pages we've dealt with just a sampling of life situations that require coping. Obviously, we cannot list all of them. However, we can develop a positive attitude that will enable us to confront any and all of them from a position of strength.

Each triumph is a bit of light. Sometimes we may find ourselves engulfed in darkness. Let us remember, just a bit of light can banish a great deal of darkness.

Perhaps this is why the first Divine Utterance of Creation was: "Let there be light."

Other titles by
Rabbi Abraham J. Twerski, M.D.
published by Shaar Press and ArtScroll/Mesorah:

Dearer Than Life

From Bondage to Freedom — A Passover Haggadah

Getting Up When You're Down

Growing Each Day

I am I

Lights Along the Way

Living Each Day

Living Each Week

Not Just Stories

Positive Parenting (with Ursula Schwartz, M.D.)

Self Improvement? — I'm Jewish!

Smiling Each Day

Twerski on Spirituality

Visions of the Fathers/Pirkei Avos